1

Retail Fashion

MASTER DATA MANAGEMENT

Charles Nesbitt

ISBN : 9781543165876

Also by Charles Nesbitt

FUNDAMENTALS FOR SUCCESSFUL AND SUSTAINABLE FASHION BUYING AND MERCHANDISING

*

FUNDAMENTALS FOR FASHION RETAIL STRATEGY PLANNING AND IMPLEMENTATION

*

FUNDAMENTALS FOR FASHION RETAIL ARITHMETIC, ASSORTMENT PLANNING AND TRADING

*

FUNDAMENTALS OF FASHION RETAIL, TECHNOLOGY, MANUFACTURING AND SUPPLIER MANAGEMENT

*

THE COMPLETE JOURNAL OF FASHION RETAIL BUYING AND MERCHANDISING

*

RETAIL FASHION MERCHANDISE ASSORTMENT PLANNING AND TRADING

RETAIL FASHION PROCUREMENT TEAM ROLES AND PROCESSES

*

RETAIL FASHION ARITHMETIC

*

RETAIL FASHION SUPPLIER MANAGEMENT

*

RETAIL FASHION SCENARIO AND STRATEGY PLANNING

*

RETAIL FASHION MANUFACTURING AND TECHNOLOGY

Contents

PREFACE 5

INTRODUCTION 6

   Retailing 6

   The retail players 7

THE PROCUREMENT TEAM 8

   Designers 8

   Buyers 9

   Merchandisers 12

   Technology 14

THE SELLING OPTIONS 16

PROCESS FLOW OF KEY RETAIL ACTIVITIES 23

MASTER DATA MANAGEMENT 23

   Building the range plan 28

   Volume and choice balance 34

   Style and shape proportions 36

   Pricing structure 37

   Colour range 38

   Size architecture 39

ORDERING 43

CRITICAL PATH MANAGEMENT 47

SUPPLIER PERFORMANCE MANAGEMENT 49

PRODUCT ALLOCATION 52

REVIEW AND ACTION OPTIONS OF IN SEASON TRADING 55

   Process of comparing the actual performance in relation to the plan 55

CONCLUSION 57

PREFACE

The process of buying and selling in some form or other of goods has been with us since time immemorial. Often when one stands in bewilderment in an elegant shopping mall and wonder how all the stores are able to effectively seduce the many shoppers trawling the wide corridors to readily part with their well-earned money while at the same time enabling them to possibly enjoy a wonderful social experience.

The plan of offering goods to the potential customer is a complicated one and is a science that involves many players whose individual contributions slot seamlessly together and are so perfectly co-ordinated that it provides the perception that it is the result of one individual concerted effort.

It will be illustrated as to how the relationships of the major functions that intertwine from the conceptualisation of a product through to the presentation of a finished garment to the potential customer and in doing this demonstrates how the key areas such as buying, merchandising, technology, production, design, logistics and selling each with their unique specialised operations manage to achieve this.

The book endeavours to try and outline the basic key principles and mechanisms by which this happens and should be helpful to students, people in retailing and those who are maybe considering a career in the industry. For those who already are part of the fashion buying and merchandising community this book will be beneficial in that it provides a complete simplified overview of all the integral activities and roles that go to make up the topic and thereby will provide a broader insight into their own career.

The material of the book, other than that specifically referenced is the result of the author's own exposure to the subject during a career spanning thirty five years at a major retail organisation in Southern Africa, the support from colleagues, mentors, interaction with suppliers and own research. There has been some cross referencing to other books or technical material but the book focuses largely at a higher level on the key principles, concepts and theories and hence there is none or very little mention of retailers by name or technological packages for some key activities such as planning, allocating, critical path management, logistics and the like.

The fundamental purpose is therefore to provide the basic background that goes into the operational and technical aspects which can be universally applied. While there is merit and great benefits in the use of sophisticated technical packages that live off a common database and also integrate with one another, sadly often the prime emphasis becomes more one of mastering the system and promotes the tendency to live in a silo environment. As a result the importance tends to be focused on that single facet that the system serves rather than the broader picture. The fact that there is a relatively limited amount of material that generally describes the practice commonly known as retailing as an end to end process considering the enormous size of the industry is one of the motivating reasons for the documentation of this book.

INTRODUCTION

Retailing

Retailing is the offer of goods or services for sale by individuals or businesses to an end user. The channels by which these goods reach the final user may vary considerably and arrive via different sources such as wholesalers, trading houses or directly from the manufacturer and there are equally many differing variants in the way the goods are put on sale. Historically it is more likely that shopping would have been done at the village or town market, in a high street shop or at the "mom and pop" store which evolved over time into mass retailing stores that are often housed in shopping malls supported by smaller line shops.

More recently with the advent of the computer utilising various platforms such as the internet or social networks, shopping on line is growing exponentially using electronic payment methods with delivery via the post or with a courier man knocking on the front door of the customer bearing their purchase relatively shortly after the transaction has been processed.

The products that are put on offer will be determined by the demand to satisfy a need in the market place. Broadly the merchandise may be categorized into food stuffs, hard or durable goods such as appliances, furniture and electronics and soft goods that have a limited life span typically clothing, apparel and fabrics. Whatever the nature of the product, the key objective will be to acquire and sell the product at a price that will be more than it cost to bring it to the place of offer and thereby make a profit.

Supporting activities such as the storage, movement of the goods, technology, and marketing will endeavour to ensure that the form, function and profit objective is maximised.

In an effort to put in perspective the activities and interaction between the various functional players and their dependency and integration with each other for the end to end process of the product workflow is broadly depicted in the diagram below

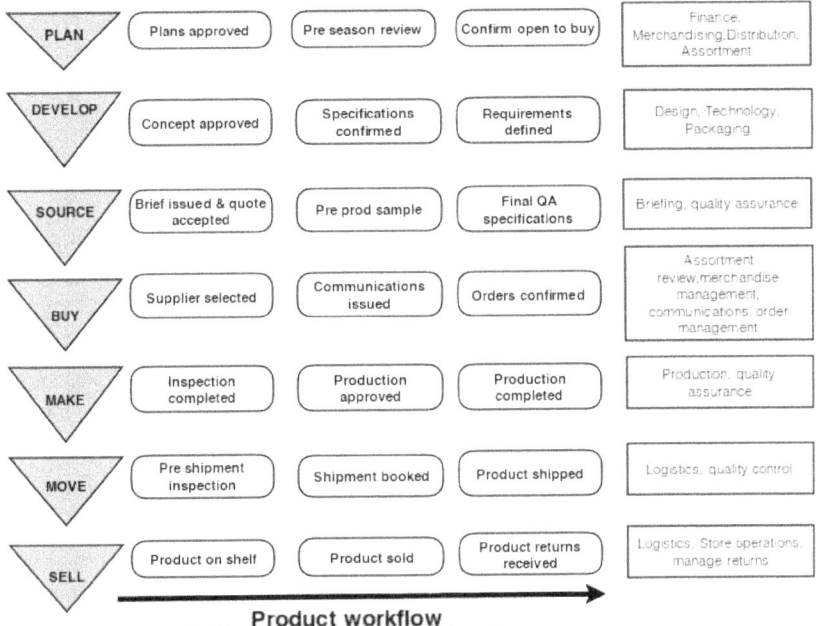

Product workflow

The distinction between supply chain and value chain should be clarified in that it is frequently misunderstood and the interpretation is varied.

Simply put, supply chain is the processes and activities that take place from conceptualisation of styles through to the procurement of raw materials and production process to the logistical operations and the eventual delivery to the end user. The value chain component is the inclusion of those functions that support the supply chain process such as the marketing philosophies. Human resource management, and consultancy resources.

The intimate details of the roles will be exposed in the future chapters as the science of retailing is explored in greater detail.

The retail players

The saying "no man is an island" holds true in many spheres and this is certainly the case in the world of clothing retailing.

Various players, each with very different specialised skills are amalgamated together to deliver a completed outcome which is that of presenting product for sale to potential customers. These players are often very diverse not only in the activities that they perform but also in their personality traits which they possess. The key to a successful team is how maturely the interaction takes place and the mutual respect that every member has for each other's roles.

Below is a brief synopsis of the main player's roles and their dependency and integration with each other. The intimate details of the roles will be exposed in the future chapters as the science of retailing is explored in greater detail.

THE PROCUREMENT TEAM

The foremost players in the clothing and apparel procurement team consist typically of the following members and are described in broad terms.

Designers

Designers have a deep insight into the market they are targeting through the analysis of the changing trends and use these to provide creative direction and develop product designs for the buying teams to consider.

Usually these participants tend to think out of the box and their creative minds can challenge some of the comfort zones of other team members. What must be kept top of mind is that they need to consistently apply their intellect way ahead of time as to what they think the customer requires as opposed to their personal desires.

Typically the character traits which they will possess are that they are independent, spontaneous, extroverts, driven by ideas and are confident by nature.

Although the general perception of the word "designer" conjures up a vision of those who work at couture level, the reality is that it also includes those who are involved in creating ranges which may also be exclusive but will be more widely available and therefore can be considered as having been mass produced. Their choices will be influenced by the type of retailer they work for or the product category that they design for. The more traditional retailer which serves predominantly mature customers will be less influenced by radical fashion swings which in contrast will definitely affect the younger market's high fashion boutiques more rigorously.

Work is done at times under enormous pressure to meet critical deadlines, tough meeting schedules and involves frequent international travel. It is not surprising the perception is often one that they live a life of glory and glamour but contrary to this belief the reality is that it is not as extravagant as made out to be.

The fashion and trade shows, whether they be for yarn, fabric or garments are tiring affairs requiring hard work and stamina as is the shopping for appropriate samples, researching fashion magazines, the use of forecasting trend agencies, internet and blogs and out of all of this they need to possess the ability to then distil the emerging trends to create a storybook that will best suit their organisation's customer profiles.

The designer lives with the constant strain of knowing that their level of success will be measured by the eventual amount of money rung up at the till and getting the styling direction wrong or overextending the life of a particular look could have severe financial implications, especially in the cases where volumes are high.

The real challenge is to convince the buying teams and senior management to buy into their vision and have the confidence that what they have in mind will be commercially acceptable to the customer. The designer cannot ignore the technical aspects of the garment production as many problems can be evaded if these are taken cognisance of during the design process.

Retailers in the southern hemisphere do have the advantage that their seasons follow those of countries in the northern hemisphere which allows them to tap into the more successful designs that are trading in volume. However, with globalisation this is not always as clear cut as it was in previous years and the ability to follow as close to the season as possible requires techniques that facilitates the shortening of lead times and attempt to get the product to market as quickly as possible. The advent of communication technologies such as satellite television, internet and social media have brought exposure to different cultures, sports, films, lifestyles and trends such as those generated by specific events, health drives, environmental awareness and technology platforms that can have significant impacts on fashion which sometimes happen at very short notice.

A very important aspect is that the designer must adhere strictly to, is that of copyright. Instances have occurred that other competitor's garments are copied almost identically whether it be by style, print or design. Invariably the driving reason for this is the speed of being able to turn on a replica at a cheaper price. Although it may not be practical to register and copyright every design, any infringement can still be challenged and a consequence could occur of having the offending garments being removed from display and destroyed.

Buyers

The buyer needs to have a clear understanding of the product that is required which is in line with the trend guidelines best suited to their target customer profiles, for both the high fashion segment as well as those that best serve the more traditional customer.

It is a fact is that the role of the designer and the buyer may be a bit blurred in that they research the same fashion forecasting sites and other sources of inspiration in order to put a range of garments together. Both roles must be aware of sizing, quality and costs related to fabrics, trimmings and production. To achieve this successfully they must be flexible enough to develop and buy the most suitable product that is in line with the prescribed strategy and achieves the desired profit margin in keeping with the set down targets. The evaluation of competitive activity and product ranges through regular store visits and comparative shopping provides the knowledge required to keep ahead of the field.

Effective communication and presentation skills are a prerequisite to brief and interact with suppliers as well as presenting product reviews to colleagues within their own group at all levels of seniority. With this comes the need to be able to accept criticism and resolve problems in a mature manner. The sad fact is that frequently when the analysis of the success of the range is evaluated at the end of the season, if the results are disappointing it is not uncommon for the buyer to shoulder the emotional burden of the poor performance. The truth of the matter is that the range was presented on more than one occasion to all team players including senior management all of whom signed the range off but in the final analysis they are more often than not, as is human nature, reluctant to be accept any proper accountability.

Coupled to ability to understand the wants of the customer is the sourcing of the most suitable supplier that will be selected for the specified product types in terms of their particular skills, technical ability, costing efficiency, attitude, transparency, honesty, focus on quality, communications and competitiveness while still meeting the ethical criteria that are acceptable to society.

A large part of the task will be to maintain good relations with suppliers, while at the same time being able to assertively negotiate prices with them and make sure the planned stocks are delivered on time. Communications need to be clear and specific to avoid disputes over issues which may arise through vague and confusing messages. For these reasons they need to be confident, take decisions based on results and be driven by a sense of urgency.

The buyer has to be multi-talented in that as well as being creative they also need to monitor the sales objectively and be flexible enough to react accordingly in terms of turning on or turning off production and transferring fabric and components to more appealing product styles where sales performance and fast emerging trends dictate.

What is key to be a successful buyer is the ability to work as part of the overall team and influence the rest of the team's activities which could be in the form of a managerial and developmental capacity that could also include both their peers and superiors.

The display of emotional maturity and commercial acumen within the controlled parameters as set by the merchandising arm in terms of the budgets, the number of product options and display space constraints is absolutely essential.

The same principle applies to the relationships that need to be maintained with the technical teams in regard to the use of the most appropriate fabrics which meet the product form and function demands in addition to ensuring that the brand standards of the garment are observed.

The fact that potentially the buyer together with the other retail players will be dealing with three to four seasons simultaneously at different stages for each season makes their task even more complicated. To clarify the phenomenon a bit further, the journey of this book attempts to describe the process from beginning to end for one season but while trading in the current season the thoughts and strategies are being developed and documented for two or possibly three seasons ahead followed by the range development leading up to the production taking place for next upcoming season.

The ability to absorb and interpret vast amounts of information from various sources, much of which originates from complex IT systems, can present a challenge to those who are not analytically minded. Systems have altered the scope of the traditional buyer from being a pure "touchy feely art skill" to having to develop basic technical abilities through the continual emergence of innovative systems which have become a great advantage to the role.

Some buyer's, such as those for knitwear, ladies structured underwear, tailoring and footwear will require more expert fabric and garment construction knowledge of their respective industries in comparison to individuals who select the more straightforward cut, make and trim products such as dresses, blouses and casual trousers.

As the trade environment has become more global and through information technology development it is much faster, interactive and has enabled business to be done more effortlessly from a home base interacting with many different countries. A great deal of the job is done amongst many new emerging countries which has led to a need for urgency and nimbleness in order to locate the most effective plants that meet the quality requirements, be able to assess the required technical abilities, understand the economic and cultural demands of the respective countries as well as the logistical peculiarities and government regulations that may exist.

The sourcing of production has to take on different approaches as the pros and cons of dealing internationally needs to be carefully weighed up against those of dealing with the ever diminishing number of local suppliers. A critical factor is that suppliers must be ethical in terms of labour practices, remuneration, waste management, working conditions and safety. If such conditions are not met it is counter to the interests of the retailer to be associated with such suppliers from both a moral point of view and the exposure of malpractices could lead to negative media reports and the retailer will suffer the consequences that accompany such deeds. The measurement of performance is therefore key to gauging the effectiveness of suppliers.

In larger organisations a buyer will probably be supported by an assistant or trainee buyer who will normally be a person who wishes to pursue a career in the field. They will be largely responsible for the organisation of the ranges, perform some clerical work whilst preparing products for garment reviews, monitoring the product development critical path and production milestones, liaising with suppliers and technology as well as deputising for the buyer when they are out of the office.

A point to note is that the relationship between buyers and suppliers often develops into more than a pure business association due to the fact that they spend much time travelling together and working closely with one another building ranges. Close familiar relationships frequently make it difficult to maintain a business like association for the mutual benefit of both parties and can cloud business decision making and judgment. The temptation of bribery and incentives in exchange for placing large orders may be desirous. For newer naïve buyers the rule that the supplier is not your friend should be firmly applied simply because they are more easily seduced by grandiose lunches and gifts as many have unfortunately found out the hard way when they move on and are no longer of great importance to the particular supplier.

A way of balancing the workloads or ranking of buyers and merchandisers is to evaluate the actual number of suppliers, stock keeping units or barcodes being handled by each buyer and then make comparisons regarding workload and productivity of each buyer to established benchmarks.

Merchandisers

There is a novelty t-shirt on the market which has the following statement blazon across the front panel which reads as follows – *"Merchandise Planner – we do precision guesswork based on unreliable data by those of questionable knowledge".* Although the humour can be appreciated it should be known that this statement is not too far from the truth as the success of merchandising objectives is reliant on many diverse inputs.

The merchandiser or planner applies their focus on maximising profitability from the business end. This is done largely through the analysis of historical sales and the influence of the trend direction to determine the range categories and product breakdown within the overall sales budget.

The role defines what stock levels are required to meet the preset targets such as seasonal stock turnover or forward stock covers based on the sales trends over time. Knowing these requirements, the merchandiser will determine what intake or purchase quantities are needed at any point in time in the season for the total department and each product category.

The level of the budgets will determine the quantity of options in relation to styling, colour palette, size spans, pricing structure and levels of quality per category that will best service the customer for the time that the goods are expected be on offer prior to a new variety of product being introduced in line with the strategic predetermined seasonal themes.

The merchandiser's job has to be to provide guidance to the buyer to procure within the budget parameters. In short it can be described as providing the buyer with a shopping list or range plan that allows them to go out and fill in the blanks on the plan while buying product. This activity requires the careful management of the "open to buy" which can often be a source of tension between the buyer who always tends to want more and the merchandiser who holds the purse strings. A good deal of emotional maturity and teamwork on both sides is therefore critical for a successful partnership.

Sadly the merchandising role is often branded as a dull, boring number crunching task in accordance with mathematical calculations and while it is this, it can be better described as a creative manipulation of numbers. This task is highly rewarding when positive trade results are achieved or alternatively equally as depressing when these do not materialise. The role can be likened to that of a husband who places his entire salary on a dead cert horse at the races which was by no means appreciated by his wife. However when the horse won he was similarly unpopular for not putting more money on the horse!

Like the buying role, the merchandiser deals with different activities simultaneously as part of the team across a number of seasons and therefore requires high levels of multi-tasking and re-prioritising in the forward planning, problem resolution, critical milestone management, analysis and timeous action implementation.

As the actual trade takes place the results need to be carefully analysed and immediate action plans initiated in order to maximise the opportunities and minimise the levels of markdowns that erode the profits. For these reasons they need to be logical, reliable, and consistent in order to take decisions based on fact.

The regular timeous generation of reports detailing sales analysis, stock levels and forward planning needs are distributed to all team members and to senior management. Often numeric information and commercial analysis is demanded on an immediate ad-hoc basis which adds pressure to the job function and can be very disruptive to routines which in such situations requires the merchandiser to adapt quickly and effectively.

The merchandiser plays an integral role during the presentation at product reviews from the numbers perspective which influences the agreed product mix and justification of the levels of sales budgets.

A detailed understanding is necessary of the stores and the customer profile inherent to respective stores that are best met through the attributes of the ranges in terms of styling, colour and size that are put on offer within the store space constraints. The task is best described by the saying "plan each store as if it is your own" which could never be truer.

With sophisticated IT development and the availability of various software packages, some of which may be developed exclusively for the retailer, will provide quick sales analysis, production planning and afford the ability to make sound decisions based on accurate data. This information is especially necessary to give guidance to the allocator or distributor who will be sending the appropriate quantities to satisfy the store's needs as well as give direction as to the level of repeat buys for products that are trading above expectations.

Some organisational structures do differentiate the allocation function between the merchandiser who focuses on the forecasting and production planning and that of the allocator or location planner who will be responsible to distribute the product to the stores in the most appropriate combinations of styles, colour and sizes that meet the store profiles. This function can be housed as an extension within the buying division or may be part of a separate centralised group where an allocator may be responsible for a diverse number of departments. The benefits of such a centralised structure is that there could be a cost saving advantage especially where smaller departments do not warrant a dedicated staff member but added to this is a pool of knowledge which develops a highly skilled team who are able to cross pollinate information, coordinate inter departmental promotions effectively and develop consistent techniques and skills. The identification of common emerging trends will contribute to the optimisation of sales and assist in the control of stock quantities at a very detailed level and thereby maximise profits. Close connections to the departmental merchandisers is maintained to ensure that their actions are aligned to the departmental strategy and plans.

The need for the diversification of the function also makes more sense from the point of view in that where the distribution function is retained within the department it inevitably adds to the increasing workload of the merchandiser. The departmental merchandiser task has more and more been impacted on by the development, the implementation and mastering of complex and sophisticated information systems that analyse sales and stock with added forward planning functionalities.

Many such systems are able to integrate with other supporting IT platforms such as supplier performance, technological measurement, critical path management, ordering, logistical and store systems. The added management of a complex allocation system that is necessary to move the stock to stores is more and more difficult with the result that the incumbent is in danger of being drawn into concentrating on and coping with the intricate detail. As a result, the merchandiser runs the risk of losing sight of the bigger objectives as set out in the strategy and operational plans and the consequent degrading of the inherent merchant intuition becomes very real.

The merchandiser needs to effectively manage and develop the merchandising team which can, not unlike the buying role, consist of an assistant merchandiser or trainee who aspire to be a merchandiser.

The role ensures cohesion of activities that have to be synchronized based on actual sales performance through the formalised interaction with other stakeholders such as the buyers and technologists. This contact is usually in the form of regular, typically weekly, departmental meetings where corrective decisions and plans of action are agreed. Frequent association with the points of sale in stores through written communications and reports as well as formal site visits are critical to keep aligned with the customer's preferences and emerging trends and confirm that the stores are sharing the same vision of the overall strategy.

The need to guide suppliers assertively in terms of prioritisation and the achievement of deadlines is critical to meet the suitable stock requirements at any point in time, particularly in relation to peak seasonal periods or key events. For example, once winter breaks, which it does every year except the exact date is not easy to predict, the objective is to have the right stocks in place such as knitwear, thermal underwear, scarves and the like in sufficient quantities to meet the rush. The usual manner to assist in the anticipation of the weather trend is done through reference to previous years data when the weather changes happened which also help to understand variations in out of ordinary performance at particular times. The challenge is therefore to have the appropriate quantities in the stores at the vital time while the maintenance of the balance of stocks must be adequate to cater for the demand without overstocking the stores ahead of planned stock targets. Events such as Easter, Christmas, Valentine's Day and Mother's day are easier to predict and the right levels of stock can be made more accurately available at the right time.

Where suppliers do not meet the required delivery dates, the merchandiser needs to manage the consequences that have to be applied for the underperformance. This can result in some very sensitive and emotional discussions and the negotiation of penalties typically in the form of discounts, sale or return agreements or even total cancellation which will no doubt impact negatively on both parties.

Technology
Technical Teams consist broadly of the fabric and garment technologists. Fabric technologists are highly trained specialists who focus on typically woven or knitted disciplines. Specialised products such as knitwear, tailoring and footwear require added knowledge of components and specific production machinery.

A major portion of the fabric technologist's task is the development and innovation of new fabrics and the enhancement of existing products. New fibres and blends of fibres such as the blending of natural and synthetic fibres, addition of chemicals to finishing process will possibly lead to new inventions and improvements such as better washability, softer handles, easy care properties like easy to iron, crease resistant finishes, rot resistant applications, seamless or seams that are glued that allow for smoother looks particularly for under garments, the evolvement of elastane products such as lycra which revolutionised active and casual wear and the enhancement of thermal properties of winter undergarments. The success of such developments which add to the profitability as well as the form and function necessitates a close working relationship with suppliers, mills and value adders.

Garment technology have the responsibility to ensure that the make-up of the garment meets the set down criteria and the componentry like buttons, interlinings and threads are of the standard that is functional and are not inferior.

Many factories have developed specified technological capabilities that have been built around the production of a particular category of garments relevant to them which vary from factory to factory or even within the same plant. The garment technologist must understand this implicitly and exploit this knowledge to its fullest.

The relationship with the commercial team is sometimes strained as the ideal level of form and function can be challenged by the need to market the product at the most commercially competitive price.

The objective of the garment technologist is to ensure that quality is not compromised. The tasks essential to achieve this can be varied, for example, the assessment of potential manufacturers and fabric mills to ensure that the established standards are achievable, the specification of raw materials, overseeing sampling stages and ensuring that any delays which may result through the process do not compromise the delivery prerequisites.

In safeguarding that the all quality standards are met particularly through the inspection of garments, inspectors need to possess specific skills. Quality controllers should be ethical, sincere and honest, open mindedly being willing to consider alternatives, be diplomatic and tactful in their dealings with people and are able to actively observe their surroundings as well as perceive and adapt to varying situations.

The technologist has an intimate knowledge of the supplier base through historical awareness as well as from continually researching new and existing suppliers. As the sourcing specialist they have to guide buying teams in the selection of the most appropriate manufacturer for the various types of product. It is also very essential that they are conscious of the fabric prominence for the forthcoming season as dictated by the strategies and budget levels to ensure that there is sufficient capacities at the relevant mills to meet the overall demands without compromising quality.

The task of assessing potentially new suppliers is a role that may be included in the stable of the technical team or it may be hived off to defined sourcing specialists who are knowledgeable team members that recognise the strengths and weaknesses of suppliers and based on this where best to place orders accordingly.

Suppliers are assessed on various criteria such as their management infrastructure, financial stability, specialised equipment availability, fabric specialty, levels of innovation, fashion or basic production orientation, the other retailers they serve, their flexibility of cost negotiability and social responsibility policies. Other external factors that may well influence the selection of suppliers could be those like prevailing exchange rates, remuneration policies and physical locality.

In summary, the significance must be emphasised that the diverse buying teams all have to have a clear informed understanding of each other's roles and priorities and that they are aligned to ensure all their tasks are integrated to achieve the goal of delivering consistent quality products manufactured by appropriately skilled suppliers on time all the time. This is especially imperative in the case of more complex products such as corsetry, tailored garments and knitwear.

The handling, packaging, storage and movement of the product through the supply channels has to be done in such a way that the quality of the product is not allowed to deteriorate in any way whatsoever. As some product is sourced from more distant locations a newer trend is to contract the technical function out to approved independent technical service providers or to trusted garment and fabric suppliers themselves who understand and are committed to the standards required. These service providers are thereby able to approve samples, perform quality control and be responsible for the eventual release of the finished product.

THE SELLING OPTIONS

There are many ways to expose the product to the customer in the hope that they will take a positive decision during the shopping process. More often than not, the nature of the product will influence the type of channel that is selected but whatever format that the retail store takes, it remains very simply a part of the integrated supply chain whereby goods are purchased in large quantities directly from a manufacturer, wholesaler, trading house or agent to be sold on in smaller quantities to the end user.

Retailing can be done in the more traditional fixed locations like stores or markets but in recent years there has been the evolvement of more innovative ways of selling the product, a typical example being "pop up" shops whereby a temporary location is used in a busy environment which is possibly a sports event, trade show or similar location where large volumes of potential customers are present. It is also an easy way of promoting goods or the carrying out of special launches.

In the modern era of technology the internet is probably the fastest growing medium through which to sell product. Online websites now exist for all types of goods and all the major traders as well as dedicated online retailers are spending large amounts of money to set up their sites in such a way that they are very user friendly, faster and most attractive with secure, easy payment methods.

The main objectives of such sites is to enable the offer of products, create a level of trust and inspire the customer to make a purchase. The establishment of trust can be aided by the use of testimonials whereby the experience of past customers affirm the selling proposition.

Door to door deliveries at an additional fee or which alternatively may be absorbed by the retailer are carried out by sophisticated courier services from various highly efficient distribution centres. International purchases in foreign currencies are also relatively easy to do in this way and customers receive the parcels within a reasonable period of time.

Another option is that the retailer may choose to carry out picking of stock from brick and mortar stores which are in close proximity to the online customer but it should be noted that this choice does bring challenges in sustaining consistent full availabilities and maintaining accurate data integrity. Similarly, some retailers offer the facility of "click and collect" whereby the customer places an order on line and at a time convenient to them collects the order from a designated store. There are also out sourced specialised delivery services that can deliver to varied pick up points across a number of facilities which in fact could be another retailer in an area which is not related to the original source of the purchase which allows for greater ease of convenience that suits the lifestyle of the customer.

The problem that customers do have is that they are not able to try on the garments so retailers need to devise some convenient special service options such as the provision of critical body measurements to assist in the determination of an appropriate size.

The fact however remains that there are many on line shopping platforms popping up every day but the challenge remains for them remains for all of them is to convert visitors to actual buyers. In order that this is achieved effectively there must be certain fundamentals present. The landing page must be compelling consisting of great visual images and bold statements that highlight the features of the products on offer. The presentation of user reviews inspires confidence in the minds of potential buyers. The personalisation of customer accounts that based on their track record of previous purchases suggest new products that would be suited to their personal profile. What is of paramount importance is the constant striving for excellence through the products that are sold, the experience on the site, as well as the maintenance of great after sales and service.

Marketing teams utilise various types of techniques to effectively expose the product in the most attractive way to the market. Traditional channels in the form of print, radio, television, in house magazines, flyers, and point of sale material as well as the use of innovative medium such as in store digital signage as a tool when they are making purchasing decisions, permeating fragrances and suitable background music or a store branded radio station all attempt to enhance the shopping experience. The use of posters and bill boards, scratch cards and the like are still very prominent in varying formats, however in increasing magnitudes, the creative use of the electronic channels by way of websites, sms, e-mail and social media such as facebook and twitter are now very evident.

The three most popular social media platforms that are utilised to promote the business is Twitter, Facebook and Instagram. Briefly, Twitter allows the targeting the advertising according to interest categories, hashtags, promoted accounts, promoted tweets and promoted trends which allow the business to build followers through greater exposure, building brand awareness, sharing content and offering special deals.

Facebook which has a global membership of 1.5 billion is the largest platform in the world and therefore is like to provide the greatest exposure to the business. Adverts can be specifically directed to specific locations, genders, interests, workplaces, status and relationship statuses. Facebook remains a very cost effective means of advertising and if the message is accurate it can be extremely successful and effective.

Instagram is the fastest growing platform and it is estimated that at more than 45% of major brands use this platform to promote their goods. The advertisements can be done in the form of 15 second videos, and photo link advertisements. Typically Instagram is more suited to brand niche advertising and social media managers need not to tale this forum too seriously but rather see it as a way to have a bit of fun and actively interact with their community. In this way it can be seen as a tool to build long lasting relationships with the audience and the brand.

It should be noted that today's customers hop from researching products on their smartphones to viewing them physically in a brick and mortar store or ordering them online without hesitation. While this has transformed the retail experience compared to a few years ago the merchant's priorities of driving sales, enhancing efficiency and delivering the absolute service have still remained the same.

Up until recently the choice of medium was simply based on the sheer traffic volumes that were enjoyed. Fortunately the approach has changed significantly and the determining factors which influence the decision of what platform to apply is now more customer centralised in that marketing campaigns use those platforms which their target customers frequent the most. In other words the company realises that the customer data is linked to the people rather than the devices and thereby can create personal experiences across varying channels.

The systematic collection of customer data through the interactive media allows the customer profiles to be analysed and targeted in a more scientific way. Loyalty programmes are very popular and mostly reward the customer either in the form of points which can be cashed in at a later stage for the purchase or provide an immediate discount at the till point. Such programmes are not only extremely effective in significantly improving sales and profits but they also allow the retailer to interpret in detail the buying habits of the customer and consequently thereby are able to better service the consumer needs. Other benefits include providing the retailer's reputation a boost and improve on-line presence and drives additional traffic to the site and thereby gain more customers.

While shopping generally refers to the activity of simply buying a product it has become very much a recreational activity whereby a visit to the shopping mall becomes a wonderful experience which may or may not necessarily result in any purchase being made. Some malls may have added attractions such as theatres, ice skating rinks, stages for entertainment and even larger magnetisms such as aquariums and fun parks while facilities such as gyms are not an uncommon appendage. Restaurant and fast food eateries are an integral part which are often positioned in centrally located food halls where both the major brands and specialised restaurants are represented.

The dominant tenants are the major retailers who are regarded to be the crowd pullers. The main mix comprise of large food chains together with typical mass clothing retailers while other stores such as general chains provide the bulk of hard and specialist goods like electronics, appliances, stationery, furnishings, jewelry, pharmaceuticals and sports shops.

A complex combination of line shops who derive their name due to the fact that they flank the interlinking walkways between the major tenants and tend to be more exclusive in their offerings. The rentals are usually at a much higher rate and the closest adjacency to a major tenant comes at a premium. Line shops will typically include outlets such as hairdressers, opticians, beauticians, boutiques, dedicated outdoor gear retailers, accessory specialists, luggage shops, photographic stores, religious retailers selling inspirational product and even tattoo parlours. Other options include the barrow type outlets selling product such as ties and accessories and specialized delicacies.

What is also evolving to a greater degree is the presence of international chains and brands from all over the world as it has become increasingly easy for stores to open due to improved technologies and exposure both from an IT perspective as well as the use of efficient transport methodologies. It has reached a stage where very few major retailers ignore opportunities to trade internationally especially where domestic markets have become saturated and increasingly competitive. The lure of new emerging markets are great but can be challenging in terms of the differing profiles of customers and culture considerations as well as the unforeseen detection of hidden costs.

Malls are strategically positioned close to residential dense areas and the science of the mix of line shops supported by the major tenants are largely influenced by the demographics of the area that they serve. Such malls may be supported by adjacent discount shopping centres which mostly include many clothing, shoe and factory outlet stores. Factory shops enable manufacturers or traders to market over runs, rejects, problem lines at reduced prices in locations that enjoy lower rentals. Liquor outlets, hardware stores and nurseries are also frequently seen adjacent to the main shopping complex.

A factor that should be addressed in the layout of malls is the ease of shopping and the implementation of plans for the free flow of traffic which does not stress the customers particularly during peak times when the mall corridors are jam packed with people. This state of affairs is leading to an ever increasing trend towards convenience shopping where the establishment of smaller shopping centres on the fringes of suburbs dispenses with the anxiety and lessens the time required to complete the shop.

The mall has largely been the cause of the demise of the "high street" store as is evident by the many major chain stores who have succumbed. The operations have consequently closed or have relocated to the shopping centres outside the city. However, there is still a place in certain instances for these stores to remain as is seen in some cities where there is in fact a reverse trend as there is still a density of office workers as well a growing inclination to live within the city centre which has led to surplus office space being transformed into apartment blocks or new developments being constructed.

Traditional general stores and co-operatives offering a broad range of everything for the community and mom and pop family run shops who purchased from the travelling salesman most commonly found in the rural areas are now very far and few between. Centralised shopping locations consist most commonly of tenants where all the relevant chains being represented with the influx of the discount shops specialising in goods from the East, (some of which may have originated from dubious sources), are now in almost every town. This has sadly relegated these old fashioned stores to no longer being in existence.

Franchise stores offer the opportunity for individual traders to invest in a mass retail group and enjoy the benefit of the support from the chain's branding, quality products and marketing strategies. The advantage for the franchisee is that the expansion and market penetration can be accelerated with external investment and they enjoy a commission for goods sold without the risk of stock holding costs, overheads and staffing expenses. The success of a franchise venture will depend mostly on enough working capital, reliable support from the franchisor and the emotional involvement in the business of the franchisee with suitable staff in the right location at affordable rentals.

In days gone by the goods were stored in walk-in counters often being displayed behind glass and in drawers with sales assistants serving the customer from within the unit as well as manning a till stationed at each counter. While this way of serving customers was very effective from an interaction point of view it soon became unsustainable due to the demands of mass retailing and convenience for the customer.

The newer formats of stores are well lit, uncluttered and appealing to the customer. They house easy to access product which is in sufficient quantities with well demarcated information through attractive signage. Displays whether on shelves, tables or garment rails are well thought out and coordinated in cameo presentations that are lit in such a way that suggest to the customer how the product pieces can be worn together in terms of lifestyle and colouration. Displays are adjacent to complementary customer needs, for example women's skirts will be located close to the blouse displays which will be adjacent to the ladies trousers. The ladies outerwear will most likely be next to the lingerie department which will lead into ladies sleepwear. There can also be a thread of the chosen similar colour themes throughout which are being promoted at that point in time.

Focus cameo displays as created by specialist visual merchandisers are located in highly visible areas such as aisles, window displays or walls which change regularly to convey the message of prevailing stories in order to attract and engage the customer. Seasonal changes, special events, promotional activity and colour themes are typically introduced in this way and thereby sustain the impact of newness, freshness and excitement. The customer not only has a pleasant experience considering the proposition but the potential opportunity of a sale is maximised.

Pay points and change rooms are conveniently placed and the design of these units are such that they lessen the frustration that comes with the inevitable waiting periods.

Personal interaction with the customer by any staff member whether they are the sales assistants or management can never be substituted. Service remains of paramount importance in ensuring that they can illustrate to the customer the ways in which styles and colours of the different components can tastefully be worn together.

Payment methodologies are also focused on in order to ensure that the customer has an enjoyable experience and is not frustrated by the task of having to stand in long queues. Technologies are advancing at a rapid pace to minimise long queues and newer examples are in the form of a shopping basket being scanned in total which eliminates the individual handling of each product, the evolvement of the contactless card which does not require the customer having to swipe cards, provide pin numbers or sign any slips. All that is required is the simple tapping of the card against a card reader for payment to be processed. Another innovative process is the establishment of self-service pay points where by the customer checks out their own goods and thereby saves considerable time. Whatever the sophistication of the payment methodologies there is one basic requirement that retailers need to make provision for and that is having a card facility. Without such a facility they will not survive for the following simple reasons. Cards are now a global form of payment and are particularly important to international travellers. They are convenient for everyone as they minimise the necessity to carry cash and are therefore less of a security risk and should the card get lost or stolen the can be quickly cancelled via a telephone call which in itself makes them safer than carrying cash.. Card payment also enables bigger purchases, which may or may not be a good thing but research shows that customers tend to make about thirty percent bigger purchases as opposed to only using cash. Because a card leaves a trace it allows for accurate tracking of transaction history and enables more responsible management of financial resources.

For the retailer, the advantages of card facilities is that they enable real time transactions which includes reporting and reconciliation. Added to this they empower the acceleration of transactions, tighten control and security and most importantly reduce costs across the board.

The unfortunate downside is that they are a soft target for cyber criminals and therefore need to be carefully protected through disciplined usage and password or pin code control.

The need for refurbishment and revitalisation of stores and displays is an ongoing process, which although being costly, regularly presents the customer with a fresh and exciting environment to enjoy the shopping experience and avoid being faced with stale, run down and drab looking stores that undermine even the most attractive merchandise.

As with the buying teams, the selling teams also consist of a mix of skills that are coordinated in such a way that the customer has a most satisfying shopping experience.

The team is spearheaded by general manager who is the head of the store. This position maybe supported by an assistant officer and they will ensure that the overall co-ordination of all the roles will deliver the most efficient running of the operation. A classic structure that they will manage consists of commercial or departmental managers each of whom will be responsible for a segment of the store.

Their role will focus on ensuring that the displays are constantly fully stocked and that they are optimally positioned and displayed proportionately appropriate to the customer demand. By way of illustration the most popular product will normally be in the front of the racks and displayed at the eye level of the customer. The size of the display will be proportionate to the relative demand, in other words, in the ideal world a product that represents twenty percent of the sales will enjoy twenty percent of the space of the relevant display area. Exceptions to this principle may occur where the product may be bulky and will have to be pallet stacked on the floor. An example of this would be nappies, duvets and cushions.

A typical layout is reflected below.

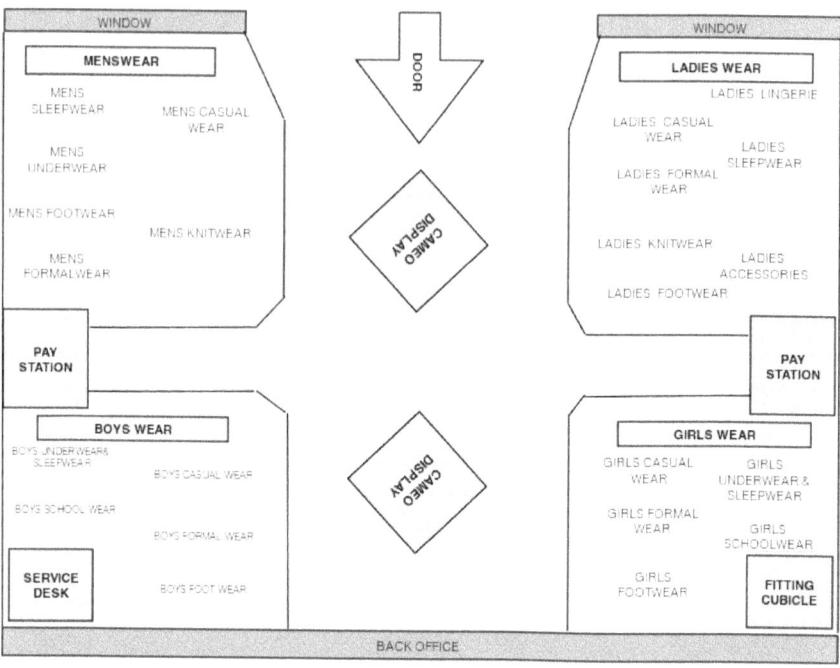

The challenge is to ensure that there is the optimum number of well trained, knowledgeable and positive staff that can best serve the customers without the overhead costs being put under pressure. The service disposition should apply for the entire shopping experience from the time that the customer is greeted at the front door until the transaction is finalised at the till point and the customer leaves the store with the added objective being that the customer will always look forward to returning to the store. Even where a sale may not transpire the offering of advice or patiently helping consider alternatives is part and parcel of ensuring that the customer will return.

Selling teams are supported by other staff functions such as the human resource officer who will be responsible for the personnel functions as well as the shift scheduling of staff. This task is imperative to ensure optimum staffing which is appropriate for the inconstant number of customers over the various times during the day, week month and year of trade. A flexible, part time work force is required which can be more than two thirds of the total store staff and because some of the hours of work are unsocial such as weekend or after normal hours variable rates of remuneration or extra time off will apply.

PROCESS FLOW OF KEY RETAIL ACTIVITIES

While a lot of activities are required from conceptualisation to the eventual offering of a completed product to the customer they do nevertheless follow a relative set sequence of events even though there may be at any point in time where they can possibly overlap each other.

In the sections that follow, the detail required for each key activity will be explored and their relationships and dependencies on each other will be highlighted.

The journey commences broadly with strategy formulation and the strategic planning for each stakeholder area, the creation of a merchandise plan through to the buying of the product within the budgetary parameters. The commercial team have the support of the technology teams to establish the technical requirements as well as the sourcing of appropriate suppliers in order to enable the production of the product.

The packaging is detailed to assist in the marketing of the product and protect the garments in transit and storage. Orders are initiated and the critical production milestones are managed in such a way to ensure delivery deadlines are met timeously.

During production the quality inspection and supplier performance management takes place and once the order is complete the products will be allocated and delivered either directly to stores or to a storage facility. In some instances there may be value added processes applied to the goods after which they will be transported to stores.

Once the goods are on offer to the customer the sales are analysed and reviewed in order to make adjustments where necessary. At the end of the season the lessons learnt are noted and applied to the strategy development for the new season.

MASTER DATA MANAGEMENT

A master data management system provides a repository of product information that enables efficient synchronisation among internal retail applications and external stakeholders such as suppliers, warehouses and logistics.

The most common processes comprehended in the master data management solutions are typically source identification, data collection, data transformation, rule administration, error detection and correction, data consolidation and the distribution of data throughout the organisation to ensure consistency and control in the ongoing maintenance and application of this information.

Management of data management is the discipline which is supported by technology that combines elements of data governance, data quality and data integration to ensure that the right data is presented to the right place at the right time.

Without a master data management system in place the result would be the need to perform numerous manual data entry processes across multiple applications. The consequence of this can be product data errors, contractual or purchase order discrepancies, longer lead times and inefficient usage of resources.

The foundation data that resides in the management data management system is static in that it seldom changes and is linked to all peer systems. The information is set up in the background and is held in a central repository and serves as the master of all merchandise and supplier information that is referenced when transactions are done and the data is sent to the relevant systems.

Broadly the information can be categorised to that which relates to the organisation, merchandise hierarchy, suppliers and time hierarchy and within these categories there is reference data which are lower levels pertaining to the various components.

Diagrammatically foundation data may be depicted as follows.

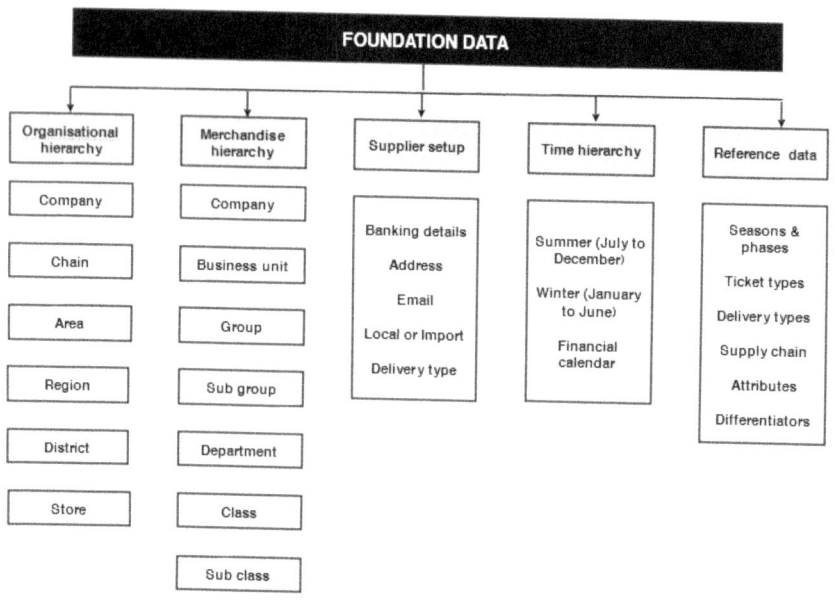

Creation of an item

In the registering of a new region, department, product, class or a new supplier with all their details for a period there will be some options which have to be chosen which reside in the system as reference data which is selected and attached to the object.

The assumption is made that in the following example a new item is being created.

The information that is attached to the item will be as follows

- **Item number – system generated sku number or barcode.**

A stock keeping unit number is assigned to each style colour and size level which enables detailed tracking of sales and stock levels that facilitates effective replenishment.

An example of such a number and associated barcode number will resemble something like

9005173048733 sku (stock keeping unit)

- **Differentiators**

Differentiators as the name implies highlights the distinguishing features that make the item be different to another product. In the creation of an item commences with the process of selecting the type they satisfy and into which group they fall and the lowest level value of the type that is qualified for.

Diagrammatically this concept is illustrated below

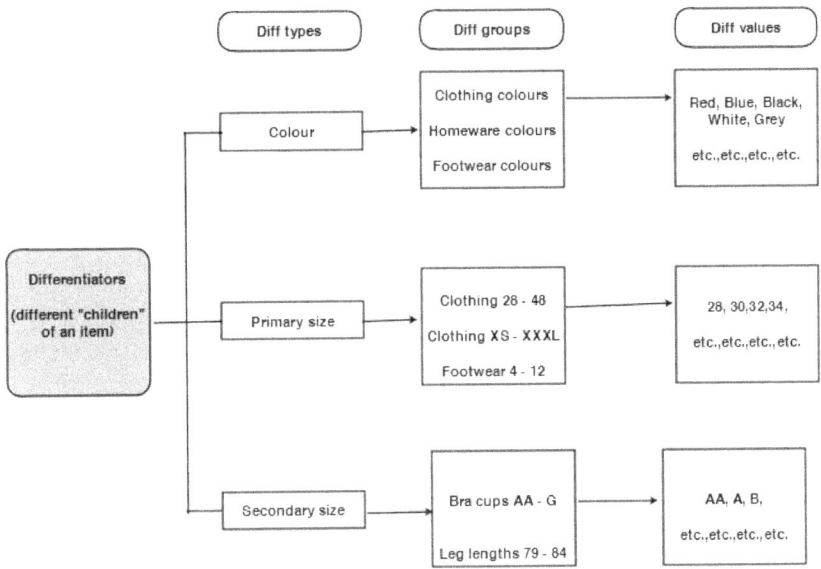

- **Attributes**
  - User defined attributes attached to items are essential to drive functionality and reporting analysis, some of which may be mandatory and other optional.
  - Examples would be whether a product is a continuity or an input product, short sleeves vs. long sleeves, tops vs. bottoms, waisted vs. non waisted
- **Seasons**

- Seasonal timing attached being spring/summer or autumn/winter
- Transitional periods between seasons

- **Supplier**
  - Local vs. imported procurement
  - Cost and selling prices will be held at item/supplier level
  - Country of origin is attached to the product and displayed on the sew in labels

- **Delivery strategy**

The delivery strategy describes how the goods will move through the supply chain to reach the end destination. The delivery strategy will be assigned to a supplier and then inherited to all items created for that supplier to determine how items will be delivered to stores.

  - Cross dock supply chain will be where the supplier picks and packs and delivers to a distribution centre which will transport the goods to stores
  - Flow through where the supplier delivers in bulk to the distribution centres where the goods will be picked and packed and despatched to stores
  - Warehouse where goods are stored awaiting a call off prior to despatch to stores
  - Vendor managed inventory where the supplier merchandises the displays in stores and delivers directly to stores
  - Direct store delivery where supplier picks and packs the goods and delivers them directly to stores

- **Cost price**
  - A cost price may be held parent level for the item which will be loaded as the same for all children
  - Different cost prices can be attached at children level where applicable

- **Selling price**
  - Is maintained at item level
  - Zone pricing can be the same or different for different regions
  - Selling prices can be the same for parent and all children or can differ, for instances larger sizes of an item may be different known as variable pricing

- **Ticket type**
  - Indicates whether the price ticket should be adhesive or swing ticket
  - Separate tickets may need to be attached where a product consists of more than one component such as shoes, children's top and bottom sold as a suit

- **Units**
  - Can be the unit of measure such as kg, items or per square metre
  - The number of products that are packed together such as a pack of six representing the allocation packs
  - Warehouse case packs that indicate the quantities that are stored in a case which must be consistent for stock counting purposes

Once all the mandatory and optional fields within the master data management system is completed the item can be approved that all the information is valid within the system. Transactions can then take place against these items.

The various types of transaction that can be actioned after the item is set up and approved is best illustrated as follows

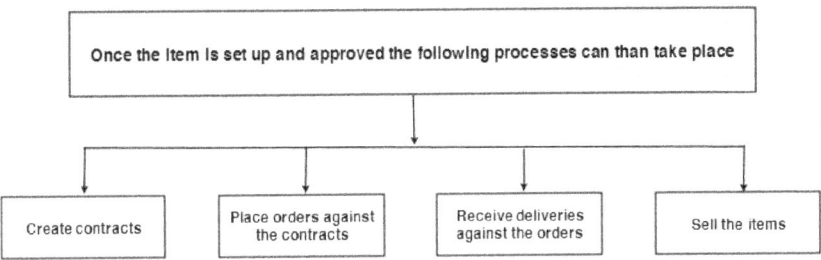

From the diagramme below it is possible to identify some of the key factors of a Master Data Maintenance system using a hypothetical department.

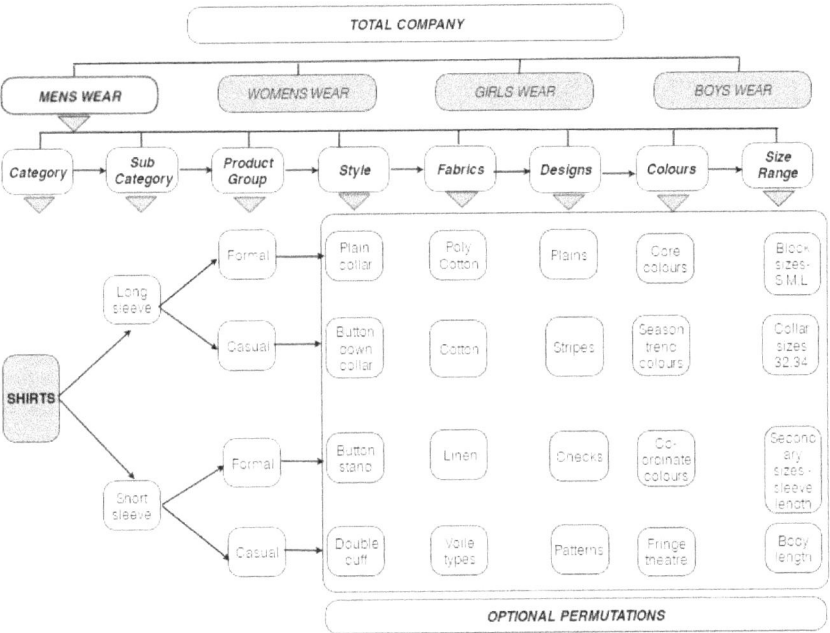

THE PRACTICAL USE OF A DATA MANAGEMENT SYSTEM

The purpose of this section is to illustrate how to marry the use of the data management system as it has been designed to cater for the various everyday key actions that depend on the utilisation of the data which is stored in the various compartments and ensure that the information is consistent and is delivered with integrity and trust.

Financial sales budgeting

A possible example of a simple line by line budget departmental summary will likely reflect the following which will be drafted utilising the information sourced from a data management system

DEPARMENTAL SALES SUMMARY

Prod No	Description	Store	Selling Price			Sales '000			Sales Units		
		Catalogue	LY	TY	% inc/dec	LY	TY	% inc/dec	LY	TY	% inc/dec
Category	Long sleeve										
Sub Group	Formal L/S										
1001	Plains/self pattern	All	150.00	160.00	6.7%	174 100	200 000	14.9%	1 161	1250	7.7%
Sub Group	Casual L/S										
1002	Prints/checks	All	180.00	199.00	10.6%	124 094	150 000	20.9%	689	754	9.3%
Category	Short sleeve										
Sub Group	Formal S/S										
2001	Plains/self pattern	All	140.00	150.00	7.1%	74 611	85 000	13.9%	533	567	6.3%
Sub Group	Casual S/S										
2002	Prints/checks	All	160.00	170.00	6.3%	124 195	150 000	20.8%	776	882	13.7%
TOTAL SHIRTS DEPARTMENT			157.32	169.43	7.7%	497 000	585 000	17.7%	3 159	3453	9.3%

Building the range plan

The construction of a range plan may commence once the financial targets are available through the product and store plans together with a store catalogue matrix. The range plan enables the drafting of a so called "shopping list" for the buying team to be able to fill in the blanks as they make their selections all of which will be stored in the data management system that will ensure wherever the data is populated it will ensure data integrity.

The purpose of the range plan is to ensure that the offer of commercial and all-inclusive product ranges meet the needs of all customers. This is done through the combination of the elements of science which covers the planning aspect and art that represents the buying function. To expand further, the scientific practice delivers the clarity of the range offer, the quantities of style and colour levels with the correct pricing policies that support structured cataloguing which meet the varying customer profile pools. The artistic involvement delivers beautiful product and style in categories offering real choice in a way that they are easy to shop. The determination to achieve a successful balanced combination will assist in the potential maximisation of sales and profit as well as undoubtedly help to grow market share.

The philosophies of building a range is the procedure of analysing the historical sales of product categories as well as heeding the lessons learnt from previous seasons and being guided by the strategic definitions. Modifications to the current range structures could be done to compensate for missed opportunities, lost sales through uncommon adversities which should be accounted for as is the need to cater for inflated sales as a result of upcoming out of the norm special events.

Stages of building the range

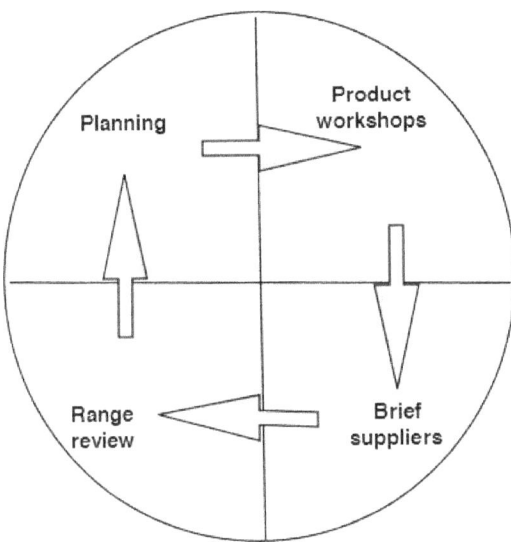

Planning begins with the range strategy document or matrix tick sheet which covers the customer choices across the period in time such as the season for six months for both the spring/summer and autumn/winter periods.

This stage is completed by the buyer and planner with reference to the group and departmental strategy.

Buyers give consideration to the historical sales, lessons learnt, customer and market shifts to determine the ideal flow of products to accommodate the continuity and input lines utilising the understanding of actual sales, customer needs and marketing plan.

Planners consider the history and lessons learnt, strategy, budgets, volumes, and the frequency of newness and catalogue shifts.

The buyers and planners then agree a final version of the range plan within the parameters of the intake budget.

Product workshops are conducted to identify the continuity items which represent the building blocks of the department, the highlighting of those products which can be seen as those that will take the department to new levels that prevent the ranges becoming stagnant, incorporating the new fashion trends which potentially could result in new shifts and ensure an appropriate level of balance between newness and traditional continuity items.

Briefing of suppliers is usually done through the compilation of a briefing pack containing quality information which enables the supplier to clearly understand the thinking of the department and get it right the first time in terms of product development. To do this effectively, the communication has to be clear and details of components, fabrics and styling features have to be simply specified. A good habit to utilise is to reference previous styles or samples.

Range reviews or final workshops are the conclusion point where the product selected is compared to the original agreed concepts and strategies to decide whether or not any changes need to be made. A cross check needs to be done to make sure that the competitive or sales environment have not altered in any significant way and plans must to be adjusted accordingly. The sequencing of the range and volumes is confirmed to ensure that all end uses are catered for, that products do not compete with each other and the categories are balanced. Lastly the range should be built from bottom up across the various groupings of stores to determine how the product will be represented across the entire chain.

The right product at the right time in the right place in the right quantities and the influences that affect these attributes is illustrated below

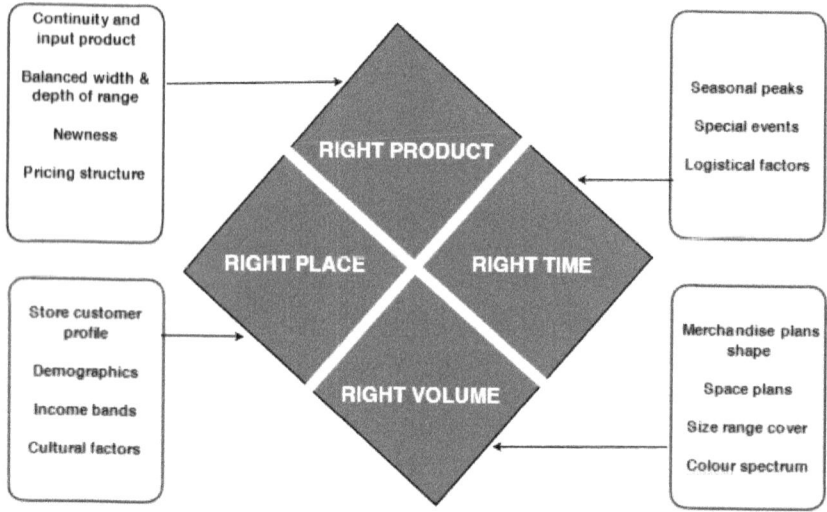

A balance of the right product mix between the basic range types and the fashion inputs has to be determined. The large volume items should be the first focus to ensure that the relevant high money takers are looked after adequately. Second is the necessity to correctly identify the characteristics of fashion forward goods for each product category in order that they best meet the respective store groupings customer profiles and reflect good relative value in comparison to other internal or external products.

The end goal is best summarised by the well-worn quote of having the right product at the right time in the right place in the right quantities.

A simple range plan model based on the guidelines reflected in the departmental line summary above is illustrated on the next page.

Department XYZ Range Plan

Product Group	Style	Colour	Stores	Cost /Input	Cost price	Sell price	Intake margin	Intake sell value	Intake units	Month 1				Month 2				Month 3				
										Week 1	Week 2	Week 3	Week 4	Week 5	Week 6	Week 7	Week 8	Week 9	Week 10	Week 11	Week 12	Week 13

Product group 1

Product group 2

Product group 3

Total Dept XYZ

For clarification of the range plan section A provides all the key data of the product in terms of product group in terms of the department's product group, style, colour, sore catalogue, whether the style is a fashion input or is a replenishment continuity line, the cost and selling price as well the resultant intake margin. The total intake value and intake units represents the "buy".

The intake value and unit buy is summarised at the product group and total level with a comparison to the merchandise intake plan which delivers the alignment status between the assortment plan and the merchandise financial plan.

Section A

Department XYZ Range Plan

Product Group	Style	Colour	Stores	Cont /input	Cost price	Sell price	Intake margin	Intake sell value	Intake units
1	1001	White	All	Cont	46.99	99.99	53%	250000	2500
		Black	All	Cont	46.99	99.99	53%	200000	2000
		Blue	Grp A,B,C	Cont	46.99	99.99	53%	160000	1600
		Purple	Grp A,B	Cont	46.99	99.99	53%	120000	1200
	2001	Beige	All	Cont	63.69	129.99	51%	300000	2308
		White	All	Cont	63.69	129.99	51%	250000	1923
		Green	Grp A	Cont	63.69	129.99	51%	100000	768
Product group 1				Intake units					12300
				Intake selling value				1380000	
				Merchandise intake plan				1380500	
2	1002	Purple	All	Input	82.81	180	54%	150000	833
		Yellow	All	Input	82.81	180	54%	120000	667
		Orange	Grp A,B	Input	82.81	180	54%	80000	444
	2002	Pink	All	Input	82.81	180	54%	170000	944
		Brown	All	Input	82.81	180	54%	140000	778
		Black	Grp A,B	Input	82.81	180	54%	100000	556
	3001	Green	All	Input	82.81	180	54%	190000	1056
		White	All	Input	82.81	180	54%	170000	944
		Grey	Grp A,B	Input	82.81	180	54%	130000	722
Product group 2				Intake units					6944
				Intake selling value				1250000	
				Merchandise intake plan				1250100	
3	1003	Purpl	All	Input	103.42	220	53%	150000	682
		Yellow	All	Input	103.42	220	53%	170000	773
		Orange	Grp A,B	Input	103.42	220	53%	120000	546
	2003	Pink	All	Input	103.42	220	53%	170000	773
		Brown	All	Input	103.42	220	53%	190000	864
		Black	Grp A,B	Input	103.42	220	53%	130000	591
	3002	Green	All	Input	103.42	220	53%	180000	808
		White	All	Input	103.42	220	53%	170000	783
		Grey	Grp A,B	Input	103.42	220	53%	130000	591
Product group 3				Intake units					6411
				Intake selling value				1410000	
				Merchandise intake plan				1410100	
Total Dept XYZ				Intake units					25655
				Intake selling value				4040000	
				Merchandise intake plan				4040700	

Section B represents the monthly and weekly intake required across time in the same or similar shape as the merchandise intake plan in units per style in units which represent the quantities that will be required to be contracted and reflected on the production plans of the relevant suppliers.

The total values are summarised in units, intake value and relationship to the financial merchandise intake plan by month and week

Section B

Month 1				Month 2				Month 3				
week 1	week 2	week 3	week 4	week 5	week 6	week 7	week 8	week 9	week 10	week 11	week 12	week 13
150	175	200	225	125	175	200	275	150	200	200	175	250
120	140	160	180	100	140	160	220	120	160	160	140	200
96	112	128	144	80	112	128	176	96	128	128	112	160
72	84	96	108	60	84	96	132	72	96	96	84	120
138	162	185	208	115	162	185	254	138	185	185	162	231
115	135	154	173	96	135	154	212	115	154	154	135	192
46	46	54	61	38	54	61	84	46	61	61	54	77
738	861	981	1107	615	861	981	1353	738	984	984	861	1230
82800	96600	110400	124200	69000	96600	110400	151800	82800	110400	110400	96600	138000
82830	96635	110440	124245	69025	96635	110440	151855	82830	110440	11044	96635	138050
708		125										
567		100										
378		67										
				803		142						
				661		117						
				472		83						
								897		158		
								903		142		
								614		108		
1853		292		1936		342		2314		408		
297500		52500		348500		61500		416500		73500		
297600		52400		348700		61600		416400		73400		
580		102										
657		116										
464		82										
				857		116						
				734		130						
				502		89						
								685		123		
								667		116		
								502		89		
1701		300		1893		335		1854		328		
374220		85000		418500		73500		408000		77000		
374010		85920		416800		73450		408020		72100		
4292	861	1573	1107	4444	861	1658	1353	4906	984	1720		
754520	96600	227900	124200	834000	96600	245400	151800	907300	110400	255900		
754440	96635	228700	124245	834525	96635	245490	151855	907250	110440	158544		

The model assumes the following.

The plan is for a department that has one continuity product group and two product groups for input fashion styles.

The catalogue makes a provision to keep in line with the product and location matrix plan.

The shape of intake across time is regulated as per the shape reflected in the merchandise sales plan.

The period being planned is for three months of a six month season.

The merchandise intake plan row is included for a direct comparison to the merchandise plan intake values for easy reconciliation to ensure that the planned buy is in line with the financial intention.

The intake margin column enables the continual monitor to ensure that the target intake margin is on track with that as deemed to be in the strategy.

The closing stock is determined using the weeks forward cover and therefore takes into account the sales values of the first few weeks in the next phase in order to calculate the closing stocks towards the latter part of the season.

The volumes of the inputs are those that are required to service the catalogue and be on offer for sale until replenished by the next style input. As in the example it is wise to keep a second smaller input to replenish initial sales as some stores will sell out quicker or slower than expected. If the full quantity is put in all at once there could be a situation where there will be pockets of stock left over which will increase the potential of mark downs while on the other hand probable sales will be lost in those stores that are depleted of stock.

The offer for sales time period is determined by the frequency of inputs. In the example above the inputs are the monthly themes and the sales period that are attributed to each style will be for six weeks after which any leftover stocks will be destined for the reduced counters or racks.

Volume and choice balance

The creation of the initial range plan reflects the quantities that have to be bought at item level by colour, in the correct size ranges, at the target mark-ups and retail selling prices. It is essential that the monetary buying amounts of the plan are aligned to the merchandise plan intake values.

The buying plan should reflect the strategy which guarantees the correct amount of selection within the stock parameters while still providing the right spread of products in the required quantities that will best serve the target customer in both style, form and function at any point in time of the season.

During the construction of the plan, the principle that needs to be adhered to is that the merchandise plan must guide the buy with the customer top of mind. Lessons learnt from previous seasons need to be analysed and equally applied to both the basic continuity lines as well as the high end fashion products. Fundamentally it is also important to get the right balance of the correct number of choices in quantities that enable the guarantee of basic lines in depth without impeding the introduction of newness.

It happens often that too much emphasis is placed on the fringe or peripheral lines, or there is excessive similarity in characteristics and price offerings that can disrupt the balance. The emotional wishes of the buying team and suppliers can also have an influence on a distorted balance being achieved and should be guarded against.

The range plan which represents the assortment of products developed within specific categories must represent the organisation of the business and therefore should be balanced across the width and depth of the structure.

The width represents how broad the choice of product is while the depth represents the quantities required to cover the number of sizes and colours including the amount of price points within the product categories. It is probably easier for niche retailers that focus on a narrower customer segment of the market to best be able to serve the both the depth and width demands of their market.

The difficulties that retailers are faced with in striking the right balance of width and depth of ranges is that of presenting real customer choice while at same time optimising the return on investment. In other words, there is the need to attract customers by maintaining a level of newness and fashionability without compromising the traditional or core customers and especially the high volume sellers. It is therefore critical that the buyer has a clear vision of the marketing position and understands the target customer though continuous research which provides the confidence to determine as to what should or should not be kept in the range.

The other challenge of having a too broad choice of styles is that the decision making process becomes an effort to select a product and diminishes the pleasure of the shopping experience.

The volume and choice balance emphasis that the customer expects to find new styles in their size in a variety of colours can be illustrated as follows.

Style and shape proportions

The styles that will make up the range structure are dictated by history, the strategy guidelines and direction provided by the design or trend teams.

If one considers the thought process of a customer when a selection is being made, the first feature that she will be attracted to is the style. If the style does not meet the required taste level it will be ignored. The criteria that will influence this choice may not necessarily be the level of fashionability but also the practicality of the garment in meeting the required functionality, examples of which are sleeve lengths, belted or unbelted waists, lengths, neckline or any other feature that will allow the customer to feel comfortable and confident to wear.

Multiple choices form the basis of range plan structure and ensure that all customer preferences are catered for. Another need that has to be provided for is the availability of styling and colours that can be easily coordinated with other product styles within the same or other departments.

Consideration also needs to be given to the cross co-ordination of fashionable items being supported by core product. An example would be a fashion blouse including the core shades in the design or print that would go happily with a basic core skirt in complimentary fabric types. The implementation of this strategy is important as too much deviation from the core pillars will reduce the product relevance and could result in a deterioration of market penetration.

Pricing structure

It is absolutely essential to consider the structure or architecture of pricing across the range in order that a consistent balance is maintained between the good value, mid and luxury price points. Added to this is the controlling of the price movement from one season to the next. The rate of increases or decreases need to be measured on a like for like basis whereby the change in price of identical products is compared to an acceptable overall rate such as the consumer price index while still maintaining the margin targets. Other products should also represent good value in comparison to similar products in the market place.

The philosophy and pricing strategy of the retailer will dictate the balance of price groups dependent on the customer segments that they serve. Probable examples would be where a discount value chain will have about ninety percent of product in the low value band while the middle price type of retailer will have possibly forty percent low price goods with the bulk of products falling into the mid-price range at about fifty five percent. Top end luxury retailers will commonly have in excess of ninety percent of prices falling in the high price range.

A pitfall that needs to be avoided is a scenario where critical price points are maintained through harsh negotiation tactics for more than one or two seasons as it could happen that it will eventually reach a point that without an increase it may become no longer viable for the supplier to manufacture. A decision to then move the price to a realistic level could result in the customer resisting the purchase as a result of the perception that the price is excessive in relation to the previous season. Credibility may also be lost as there may be great difficulty in justifying the narrower gap difference between other products within the range and they in turn could be interpreted to represent poor value.

Extreme deep cut promotions may have a similar impact and the danger exists that the balance of the margins may become distorted. An overall anticipated intake margin is based on planned quantities but in reality is rapidly lessened where repetitive turn-ons of the lower margin product takes place.

A factor that must be considered is the effect of the price movement on unit volumes and whether or not the reduced quantities will still service the store catalogue sufficiently to maintain good continuity. If this is not the case it may require the rationalisation of the number of customer choices offered or a restriction of the store catalogue for the product.

A tactic that retailers frequently resort to in terms of a psychological influence is the selection of the number of price points as well as the pricing terminology. For this reason price points such as 99.99 presents a better perception of value than if the product was marked 100.00. This technique however must be handled with caution as for high ticketed items it is better to present 300.00 rather than 299.00 as this may deliver a message of perceived deviousness. In terms of the gaps between price points, the wider they are among the product groups the better is the value perception. In cases where the customer is bombarded with too many price options it becomes increasingly difficult to assess the value variance between products.

Retailers sometimes apply regional pricing where the income status of customers differ. The result is that customers in the poorer areas enjoy a discount that is subsidised by those in the more affluent areas. Similarly there are unscrupulous retailers who launch a product at an unrealistic high price and after a short period reduce it to a price that delivers a normal margin but is promoted aggressively as great value. These practices once exposed are not well received by consumers and become great topics of discussion on social media.

Colour range

The second determining feature of the product that will influence the purchasing decision will be the colour. Colour is the first element of newness and trend direction that is displayed. Many season's ranges can fail through poor interpretation of the seasonal colour trend. How the colour themes are flowed across the seasons is important as is the harmony that exists with not only the colours within each individual product range but also with the overall look of the store. The visual impact is important in that it transmits a subliminal message to the customer through a fine balance of fashion colours to those that the customer prefers.

Core colours should be banked first even though they may not always be the most exciting. A wise retailer once said "white is a business" and this certainly holds true for black, grey, navy, beige and brown year in and year out. The trending themes such as lilacs, pinks, yellows are more often than not linked to the prevailing trends and will dictate the seasonal themes from month to month. There is a place for the high risk edgy colours such funky pinks, shocking purples and burnt oranges as they provide the theatre even though they may not deliver the best returns.

In order to achieve the best variety it is important to ensure that the planned colour spectrum is reflected as a whole by assigning different colours across the diverse styles in the range with the overall proportions meeting the targets of the strategic intent.

Examining the table below it is evident that the plan is not aligned to the strategic target and therefore a revisit to the proportions will be required to bring them in line with the objective.

NUMBER	COLOUR	UNITS	LY	UNITS PLANNED	TY	TY TARGET
1	White	250	19%	356	25%	28%
2	Black	430	33%	356	25%	25%
3	Stone	130	10%	178	13%	15%
4	Khaki	200	15%	178	13%	12%
5	Red	250	19%	178	13%	10%
6	Pink	40	3%	178	13%	10%
	TOTAL	1 300	100%	1 424	100%	100%

Size architecture

As has been highlighted previously, the first attractor to the customer is the style and then colour but the reality remains that the choice will only be complete if the size is available in the wanted style and colour. For this reason many retailers will display their offerings by size so as to minimize the frustration that results when the size is not available in the desired style and colour.

The need to minimise the non-availability of particular sizes is the main reason as to why special attention should be paid to the careful planning and analysis of size profiles.

It is logical that stores have differing size profiles which are driven by the local demographics, shopping patterns and cultural preferences. For this reason the product groupings and styling features need to be carefully assessed. Typical examples would be that possibly in the rural areas customers may be genetically of a larger stature than their counterparts in the cities and could also have a more conservative attitude than the adventurous city slickers. Religious beliefs may also have an influence where certain parts of the body such as arms need to be covered.

As with the top down and bottom up merchandise planning principle we need to determine the overall national size curve for a department, product category and product in order to place the full combined order with the supplier.

Similarly the accumulated store size profiles have to be derived and aligned with the product size profile in order that allocations can meet both the product and store needs.

The size analysis for small, medium and large emphasis size stores will require differing size ratios for each group.

By way of illustration

The department requires total of 6200 units. Based on historical and trend analysis the target size ratio will represent.

	SMALL	MEDIUM	LARGE	X-LARGE
TOTAL ORDER	1 000	1 500	2 500	1 200
SIZE RATIO %	16%	24%	40%	20%

There are three product styles which may or may not be ordered from the same supplier but each will be in the form of a separate order or contract. Because of the different characteristics of each style, the size ratio requirements may be different.

The quantities in the table below will reflect these separate style orders

STYLE	SMALL	MEDIUM	LARGE	X-LARGE
STYLE A (basic for average customer)	300	500	600	400
% RATIO	17%	28%	33%	22%
STYLE B (larger for fuller figure)	200	600	1 100	800
% RATIO	8%	22%	40%	30%
STYLE C (petite high fashion style)	600	900	400	200
% RATIO	29%	43%	19%	9%
TOTAL	1 100	2 000	2 100	1 400
% RATIO	17%	30%	32%	21%

It is not uncommon in women's sizing designed to fit diverse body shapes to carry different descriptive names. Such variations include the height of a person dependent on the torso or back length, whether the bust, waist and hips are straighter which is usually more relevant to teenagers or curvier for mostly adult women.

Examples of such descriptive categories are commonly misses sizes, junior sizes, women's or plus sizes, petite, junior petite and the like.

In order to cater for the varying size silhouettes of individual stores the relevant size ratios pertaining to the particular stores have to be applied. A practical way of doing this can be done by grouping stores with similar size profiles together and utilise these groupings for planned allocations.

A simple working example is outlined below.

Style A – Basic for average customer

Total units are 1800 units

Assume that the total proportions for the store groupings are

Small size emphasis stores	25%	440 units
Medium size emphasis stores	55%	
		990 units
Large size emphasis stores	20%	370 units

Based on historical analysis and trend assessment assume that size % splits across the size range for the various store size profiles will be as follows.

	Small	Medium	Large	X-Large
Small size emphasis stores	22%	27%	32%	19%
Medium size emphasis stores	15%	31%	32%	22%
Large size emphasis stores	13%	21%	37%	29%

The results displayed in the table below reflects in what proportions the total ordered quantity of 1800 will be allocated to meet the size profiles of the individual stores.

	SMALL	MEDIUM	LARGE	X-LARGE
SMALL EMPHASIS STORES	97	119	140	85
SIZE RATIO	22%	27%	32%	19%
MEDIUM EMPHASIS STORES	153	305	320	209
SIZE RATIO	15%	31%	32%	22%
LARGE EMPHASIS STORES	50	76	140	106
SIZE RATIO	13%	21%	37%	29%
TOTAL	300	500	600	379
SIZE RATIO	17%	28%	33%	22%

A typical overall size curve can be illustrated using a Bell type curve

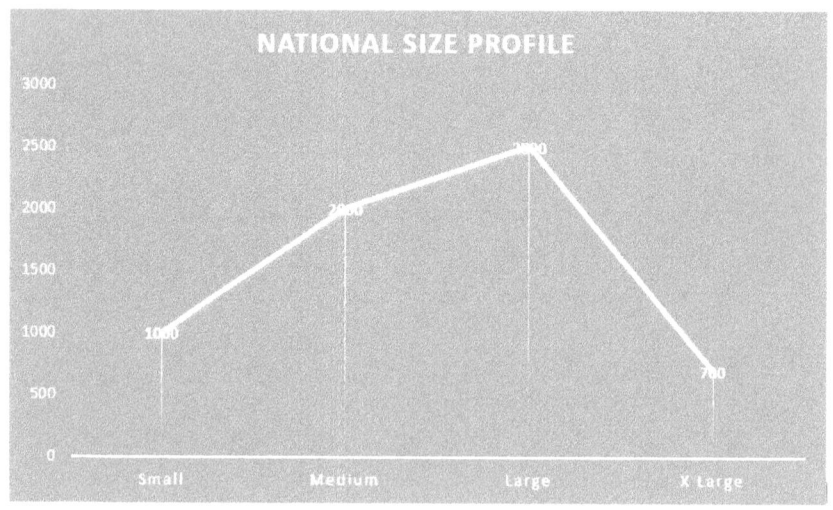

While the above represents the overall size curve this will have to be equivalent to the sum of the individual product categories size curves.

For simplicity we can assume that this overall curve is made up of three product types which are a basic type with medium size emphasis, a style for the fuller figure and a high fashion smaller size emphasis requirement. These in turn need to service stores that are size small emphasis, size medium emphasis and size large emphasis profiles.

In conclusion a check list should be drafted which confirms that all the deliverables expected from the range plan are adequately covered. These would include the confirmation of the presence of key looks and trends for the season, that all the end use options are available for the customer, that the range has a look of freshness, the assortment includes the expect to find products and does not contain any duplications.

Validation is required to ensure that the strategic intents of the product group, supplier, sourcing team and designers have been met and lastly that the margin target is achieved.

ORDERING

After the negotiations are completed and the decision to award the production of a style to the supplier is taken, an order has to be drafted to reflect the commitment to the supplier.

The signed order for the supplier is created and placed by the retailer for the entire season in the case of a continuity product or possibly monthly for input styles. It is imperative that it must be done timeously to ensure the required completion date is realistically achievable and the production lead time required will be determined by careful critical path production management.

While the order is in essence a contractual document it will be subject to the overall terms and conditions that are entered into in a memorandum of agreement that is drawn up separately when a manufacturer is appointed as a certified supplier. Production can only commence once the final approved order is in the possession of the supplier.

The contract or the order is the document that details the terms by which the retailer takes ownership of the goods in exchange or payment of an agreed price.

The timing of orders is done according to the range plan guidelines and each supplier will be provided with an extract specific to them for the season. This production programme will indicate the style details, quantities, size ratios and colour specifications which will enable them to plan the production capacity and will be used as the point of reference during follow up production progress meetings. Each style will also have a corresponding style specification sheet which confirm the costs, pack quantities, labels and tickets, wash and care details, testing requirements and the fabric as well as component information.

Orders may be amended where required. These adjustments are normally for quantities, dates, prices and size ratios. The changes need to be recorded on the contract and refer to the date of the alteration as well as the nature of the change.

It is advisable that any style changes require the order to be cancelled and be replaced by a new order as in essence it is a different product.

The order can have two status phases where a pre-production contract enables the supplier to procure fabrics, components, labelling and packaging and make a pre-production or pre shipment sample which will be submitted to the retailer for approval. The sample will serve as the set standard of quality that will be referred to should any disputes evolve in production or in stores.

Production may only commence once a final approved order is received by the supplier.

Documented programmes of continuity lines for the full season may serve as an authorised arrangement from which the supplier will be able to order the raw materials and components but they will only be able to commence production of agreed quantities, for example, for six weekly time periods upon the receipt of an approved contract. This gives the retailer the flexibility to make adjustments based on current performance. Such amendments may take the form of changes to quantities, size ratios and colour quantities.

Dependent on whether the supplier is local or offshore the delivery requirements need to be clearly outlined with all relevant contact details, delivery stipulations, carton markings and delivery addresses.

In the case of a local supplier, delivery is normally to a designated warehouse at an approved time. Off shore suppliers may have to deliver to an offshore centralised consolidation centre where the goods will be amalgamated by shipping agents into containers prior to shipping. Payment will be made in the foreign currency and will be dictated by the international commercial (INCO) terms applied.

A typical order for imported and local products will probably be as follows

ORDER

RETAILER XYZ

ORDER NO		DATE	
SUPPLIER		ORDER STATUS	Pre production	Production
SUPPLIER REFERENCE		COMPLETE/SHIP DATE	
PAYMENT TERMS		LAUNCH DATE	
DELIVERY METHOD		PACK QUANTITY	
DELIVER TO		TOTAL QUANTITY	
		COST VALUE	
		SELLING VALUE	

SKU NUMBER	STYLE NUMBER	STYLE DESCRIPTION	COLOUR	TOTAL COLOUR UNITS	SIZE	TOTAL SIZE UNITS	COST PRICE	SELLING PRICE
100023564	12345	Basic t-shirt	White	1000	S	200	45.00	99.99
100023565					M	400	45.00	99.99
100023566					L	300	50.00	110.00
100023567					XL	100	50.00	110.00
100023568	12345	Basic t-shirt	Black	2000	S	400	45.00	99.99
100023569					M	800	45.00	99.99
100023570					L	600	50.00	110.00
100023571					XL	200	50.00	110.00

| BUYER SIGN | | MANAGEMENT SIGN | |
| MERCHANDISER SIGN | | SUPPLIER SIGN | | DATE | |

The information typically included on the order is as follows and will be stored on a data base system for any interested party that needs to access the detail.

Supplier reference number and name

Order number

Date that order was raised

Port of loading

Shipment date and launch dates

Shipping method

Method of payment

Payment terms

Point of delivery

Style number

Style description

Colour break down and quantity

Labelling instructions

Special terms or conditions of trade

SKU number

Size breakdown

Quantities

Cost Price less any negotiated discounts

Selling Price

Number of cartons

Carton dimensions

Number of units per inner pack

Number of inner packs per outer carton

Signatures of authorization to buy are most commonly those of the buyer, merchandiser and a member of senior management. The omission of any of the signatures could result in the order being rendered invalid in the case of a disagreement. A supplier signature is often the rule but the acceptance of the order is in essence the recognition of all the terms and conditions of the order.

It is not uncommon for planning production schedules or provisional orders to be handed over to the supplier prior to the issuing of an official order, particularly in the case of replenishment product where the supplier needs to plan capacity requirements, order raw materials and components but this is by no means the go ahead to commence production. Without the completed signed order no knife may be put to the fabric.

The higher level order may be supplemented by a detailed specification pack and a critical path management document that serves as an appendage to the order and reflect the details and quality references of the fabric and components, sample submission requirements, technical tests, labelling instructions, packaging reference numbers and specifications.

The buying and merchandising team will use the basic information to interrogate orders at any time to check, monitor and if required will amend the orders which may be, for example, quantity or date related. Other areas of operation or parties will also need to have access to orders in order that their activities are completed timeously to safeguard that the final completion date is met.

Technology has to utilise the detail to ensure in the process of managing the critical path that all tests, quality control during the manufacturing process, garment fittings and rail samples are completed timeously.

The finance department need to know all the costing details and terms of payment as well as the proposed selling price to ensure that there is sufficient cash flow available to enable payment and be able to monitor the achievement of the gross profit margins.

The IT departments need to be aware of all orders for the provision of the SKU numbers as well as cater for the generation of the swing tickets or labels that are attached to the garments indicating the style number, colour, size and price detail which are either sent to the suppliers in bulk or the data files are transmitted to those suppliers that have the facilities to generate their own SKU tickets.

The distribution centre must have sight of the orders in the pipeline to assess the size of proposed deliveries going forward to ensure that they are in a position to plan sufficient resources in terms of staffing, equipment, space capacity and that sufficient transport is booked to deliver the goods speedily to stores.

The space capacity requirements both in the warehouse and stores will depend largely on the packing configurations in terms of the storage outer carton which is how the goods will be stored, allocated and transported to stores and the inner packs which are otherwise known as the saleable unit that will be presented to the potential consumer.

CRITICAL PATH MANAGEMENT

Critical path management is undoubtedly one of the key philosophies that needs to be applied in production management in order to have control and knowledge of the work flow in the production of garments. This achieved by the setting up of a timeline that reflects the anticipated critical deadlines that have to be achieved in order to meet the required delivery date of the order and being completely aware of the impact of late deliveries of fabric and components on the realisation of this objective. Without the knowledge of all statuses the consequence could well be the late deliveries with the application of penalties or even worse the cancellation of orders.

Through the management the entire flow of product workflow through the view of progress from concept to completion allows the effective planning of tasks and reallocation of resources to minimises bottlenecks, identify due dates and milestones as well as highlight areas where attention is required. And thereby keep suppliers on schedule as well as encourages collaboration between the different teams. A major benefit is that critical path management allows management to move away from day to day reactive management into a more strategic management role aligned with strategic business objectives.

Ideally a critical path management tool should possess characteristics such as flexibility that enables the tool to be configured to meet the customised requirements of the user. Alerts should be built in to notify stakeholders directly through SMS, emails or pings and Information should be able to be automatically rolled up with an analytical ability to be able to drill down to prescribed levels or issues.

The interface ought to be user friendly and easy to learn, easy to update and where web based tools exist they should be compatible and easily accessible within a range of internet speeds, browsers and levels of internet sophistication that allows global interaction with suppliers in order to track the progress of the product from the sampling stage through to delivery. As supply chains grow in complexity with increased production volumes and links in the supply chain information visibility is imperative in order to facilitate complete transparency while also highlighting the ramifications of poor decision making and poor capacity management.

Some of the software tools that are available in the market place which assist in the monitoring of production progress and are accessible to all stakeholders do come at a cost and albeit expensive the benefits of the investment may well be justified.

Alternatively if the product is too expensive it is well worth developing one's own instrument even though the tool may well be cumbersome and more complex to apply but at least it will provide rough idea of the lead times required for the procurement of fabrics and components for the completion of orders and therefore In order to guarantee the on time launch of the product and the management of the path of product development. Without this the retailer ends up flying blind and often only finds out about delays from the supplier close to the expected delivery date when it is invariably too late to take corrective action. It is not uncommon to hear of the cancellation of large volume contracts worth great values as a result of the relatively low cost care labels not being available on time and thus the completion of the delivery date is compromised. It is not only the physical components that can cause issues the added value outsourced services such as embroideries, pattern making or packaging can in the same manner impact the delivery status if they are not completed on time.

Unfortunately with multiple versions of documents such as cost sheets, design samples and supplier scorecards in differing formats which provide an inadequate platform to share information can result in a lack of awareness into potential supply chain problems and an inability to provide early warnings and synchronise real time responsiveness.

All stakeholders involved in the process, which includes the buyers, suppliers, product technologists, fabric technologists and commercial management need to focus on the critical path management of the product.

The key stages or milestones which are in the main controlled by the buyers and technologists that need to be scrutinised are the style briefing and finalisation, colour approval, fit approval, bulk test of fabrics and components, approval of the pre-production sample, pre-production meetings with the supplier and final approval of the pre-shipment or rail sample prior to production at which point the product development can be considered complete and the launch date is able to be confirmed.

The monitoring of the process needs to documented and highlighted in some form in order that key players are able to measure the actual accomplishment of tasks compared to the required completion dates. If collaboration and communication is ineffective, bottlenecks are likely to occur, production and delivery deadlines may be missed, and penalties will be applied with the resultant squeezing of margins. The purpose of such reports is not only to ensure that the critical milestones are met on time but also serve as a reference for meetings to identify possible delays and decide what actions need to be taken to improve or correct the situation.

In principle the lead times are measured in weeks and the relevant dates are attached starting from launch date which represents zero days and progressively working backwards taking the time for the completion of each stage into account and ending up where the no later than date for the starting style brief stage is determined.

The format of the critical path action plan may well vary from retailer to retailer dependant on the level of detail the measurement takes place in terms of each operation.

The hierarchy of the reporting and performance measurement is usually done at style level and all the styles for a department can be rolled up to departmental level and then up to group level. These together with supplier extracts and other filters make for effective performance management of both the retail teams and the supplier.

An example of a basic critical path management tool which highlights the key milestones, time line and progress monitoring with analytical properties is illustrated below.

PRODUCT DEVELOPMENT MANAGEMENT							Style Brief		Style Finalised		Colour Approved		Fit Approved	
Supplier	Grp	Dept.	Style	Colour		Total	Complete	In-complete	Complete	In-complete	Complete	In-complete	Complete	In-complete
abcd	1	123	44445	Black	Units	1000	900	100	800	200	900	100	750	250
					%	100	90%	10%	80%	20%	90%	10%	75%	25%
					Weeks	39			28		24		11	
					Date	10-Oct			17 Dec		15-Jan		15-Apr	
Supplier	Grp	Dept.	Style	Colour		Total	Complete	In-complete	Complete	In-complete	Complete	In-complete	Complete	In-complete
abcd	1	123	55555	White	Units	1500	1300	200	1400	100	1450	50	1500	0
					%	100	87%	13%	93%	7%	97%	3%	100%	0%
					Weeks	39			28		24		11	
					Date	10-Oct			17 Dec		15-Jan		15-Apr	
Supplier	Grp	Dept.	Style	Colour		Total	Complete	In-complete	Complete	In-complete	Complete	In-complete	Complete	In-complete
bcde	2	124	55556	Yellow	Units	2000	1500	500	1400	600	1600	400	1800	200
					%	100	75%	25%	70%	30%	80%	20%	90%	10%
					Weeks	39			28		24		11	
					Date	10-Nov			17-Jan		15-Feb		15-May	
Supplier	Grp	Dept.	Style	Colour		Total	Complete	In-complete	Complete	In-complete	Complete	In-complete	Complete	In-complete
cdef	3	128	44445	Green	Units	1000	200	800	900	100	800	200	750	250
					%	100	20%	80%	90%	10%	80%	20%	75%	25%
					Weeks	39			28		24		11	
					Date	10-Dec			17-Feb		15-Mar		15-Jun	

PRODUCT DEVELOPMENT MANAGEMENT							Pre-production sample & supplier meeting		Pre-shipment sample		Launch Date	
Supplier	Grp	Dept.	Style	Colour		Total	Complete	In-complete	Complete	In-complete	Complete	In-complete
abcd	1	123	44445	Black	Units	1000	750	250	750	250	750	250
					%	100	75%	25%	75%	25%	75%	25%
					Weeks	39	8		2		0	
					Date	10-Oct	06-May		17-Jun		01-Jul	
Supplier	Grp	Dept.	Style	Colour		Total	Complete	In-complete	Complete	In-complete	Complete	In-complete
abcd	1	123	55555	White	Units	1500	1500	0	1450	50	1500	0
					%	100	100%	0%	97%	3%	100%	0%
					Weeks	39	8		2		0	
					Date	10-Oct	06-May		17-Jun		01-Jul	
Supplier	Grp	Dept.	Style	Colour		Total	Complete	In-complete	Complete	In-complete	Complete	In-complete
bcde	2	124	55556	Yellow	Units	2000	1800	200	1700	300	1900	100
					%	100	90%	10%	85%	15%	95%	5%
					Weeks	39	8		2		0	
					Date	10-Nov	06-Jun		17-Jul		01-Aug	
Supplier	Grp	Dept.	Style	Colour		Total	Complete	In-complete	Complete	In-complete	Complete	In-complete
cdef	3	128	44445	Green	Units	1000	850	150	950	50	950	50
					%	100	85%	15%	95%	5%	95%	5%
					Weeks	39	8		2		0	
					Date	10-Dec	06-Jul		17-Aug		01-Sep	

SUPPLIER PERFORMANCE MANAGEMENT

In order that supplier performance will be at consistently high standards there must be a solid foundation of core requirements in order to achieve the objective at hand. While it is important that performance is influenced by external environmental factors and the customers that are served the most influential factor that impacts the operational efficiencies is undoubtedly the management of the organisation.

While the day to day measures are important, some of which may be minor such as containing canteen costs, time keeping, rental and logistical costs and the like it is critical that management focus on the longer term issues such as staff training and development, process control, maintenance, production planning and the consistent achievement of set down performance indicators.

Such a set of performance indicators are cascaded down through the organisation and as a result each employee is constantly aware of how they are being evaluated and whether they are adequately meeting the standards for which they are held accountable. The pay structure, including bonus incentives should be in place based on the achievement of the recognised KPI's.

It is equally important that management maintain their visibility on the production floor and interact at all levels in order to keep motivation at high levels with good communication and also when they relate to retail customers they are able to do so with knowledge of the hands on challenges.

Safety has to be promoted to the fullest with respected and assertive safety teams in place that have the support of senior management, and all staff should be equipped with appropriate effective personal equipment.

Research and development departments should continually be innovating, testing and improving products while apart from a robust preventative maintenance programme the reinvestment in the company by the owners is key to maintaining regular customers and attracting new ones.

The objective of achieving zero defects and delivering optimum quality is done through the building and sustaining of relationships by continually assessing, anticipating and fulfilling stated and implied needs.

It is important that service level agreements are set up front and are understood and committed to by all. SLA's clearly define the clients can expect from service providers and outline what their responsibilities are. This ensures protection for both parties and promotes beneficial long term relationships.

The risks that can be encountered are aggravated in certain situations such as with the movement of strategic product to new plants, or existing suppliers being utilised for different types of products which they may not adapt well to. The allocation of high volumes with a minimal quality assurance infrastructure in place as well the ability to meet critical launch dates require that performance measurement is critical for early identification of any potential failure.

A tough line has to be taken on dealing with substandard delivery and quality. Data collected from various sources needs to be accurate and reliable especially where a penalty system is applied for non-performance.

Customer returns have to be analysed and criteria put in place which may result in a penalty being applied for the number of returns in the form of a sliding scale. The analysis of the most common faults also highlights the areas of quality which need to be addressed.

The late or under completion of orders or non-conformance to size and colour ratios translate directly to lost sales and can be assessed and penalized either through a direct fine or a trade discount and possibly a sale or return arrangement. A word of caution with regard to a sale or return arrangement is although the goods that are not sold after a period of time can be returned, the sales of these goods may impact the performance of other similar products that are on offer at the same time which is not always taken into account.

Late deliveries measurement ensures that completion is on time according to the critical path. A typical example of a penalty is one which is on a sliding percentage scale of discount for every week that the delivery date is missed up to a pre-determined stage after which the order faces cancellation.

Lead times can be measured based on the time taken for the supplier to deliver to the retailer's back door. A realistic number of days can be set as a tolerance for the delivery of product based on mode of transport and distance from the retailer thereafter penalties may be activated. It does happen that the supplier may report the full availability of product but in reality part of the order may still be in production and the delivery may take place in the form of a number of split drops which would be unacceptable and is almost equivalent to fraud.

Order fill percentage represents what was actually delivered in comparison to what was ordered. Any deviation to this translates into lost sales from the lowest size level as the retailer is not receiving what was ordered.

Ticketing must be accurate as an incorrect ticket which is scanned in will be captured erroneously on the stock data base and sales at the till point will be incorrect thus distorting the product's data integrity which will only be rectified once a physical product count is completed. Sample checks upon receipt of product will help identify such errors and enforce the implementation of a penalty system. Often the attachment of incorrect SKU tickets could be as a result of poor communication and disciplines between the retailer and supplier, poor control at suppliers or non-destruction of old SKU tickets at times of a price changeover.

The advantage of a controlled performance management system is the quick identification of poor performing suppliers. The more efficient suppliers welcome the performance measurements as it assists supplier management to more effectively manage their business, assign accountability and also be able to assess their contribution to sales performance and strive to benefit from the advantage of incentive schemes applied by the retailer where they exist.

It is not surprising that the garment manufacturers are in turn also applying penalty systems and clauses in the contracts with their raw material suppliers such as the fabric mills and trimmings suppliers.

It is preferable that a reporting system is entrenched and is published on a monthly basis to the supplier and the internal buying groups. Such reports form a good basis of discussion in meetings with the supplier and alerts the buying team to potential problems that may be evolving. It should therefore be no surprise to the supplier if the need to apply penalties is necessary as sometimes the monetary value of the penalties could pose a major financial risk to a supplier.

Supplier meetings where qualitative feedback and their performance measures are discussed encourages commitment between the two parties and promotes collaboration. At such meetings the sales performance of the products specific to the supplier is analysed and understood. This may lead to the formulation of action plans where required and may include cooperation and coordination of marketing activities which could comprise of cooperative advertising and media campaigns. Part of the discussion would include the sharing of information regarding consumer, product, market trends and new innovations.

PRODUCT ALLOCATION

Once production is complete the supplier will advise via a report what volumes by size and colour are complete and packaged ready for dispatch to the addresses as stipulated by the retailer.

In a perfect world the intake will match the volumes as indicated on the intake line in the original plan as highlighted earlier. However, sales will never be exactly as expected as the customers do not have prior knowledge of the plans and will always buy differently. Coupled to this the amount of over or under production due to a reject factor could result in availabilities being higher or lower than what the supplier was meant to make and therefore the actual closing stock at the end of each period will definitely vary to the expectation. Markdown values are also continually different to that planned.

Stocks and sales are the anchor targets that are consistently aimed for with the intake being the balancing variable to bring the plan back in line. In the hypothetical exercise below done for Month 1 of the plan it is illustrated as to how the intake is manipulated over the four weeks of the month in order to meet the original stock targets.

It must be noted that the monetary intake requirement needs to be converted to units at the style/colour level to enable the stock availability to be allocated and distributed.

The allocation of product from the availability reports provided by suppliers or stocks stored in the warehouse takes on two methodologies. The input type products, usually for seasonal launches or fashion styles are described as "push" products while the continuity product which is replenished in empathy to sales performance are known as "pull" products where allocations are triggered by minimum stock level points and stopped by the maximum stock level thresholds.

The key differentiators of these types of products are that "push" styles cater for peak sales before being replaced. These styles attract a higher markdown volume as they are removed off display once the range becomes broken as they need to make way for the new themes that the replacement input styles bring.

"Pull" styles determine the requirements based on replacement of actual sales to a pre-determined build to level of stock. The calculation of the quantity of stock required will be the be determined by the amount of intake needed to meet the stock target that is either dynamically determined by the set weeks sales forward cover or is maintained at a static level over time.

"Pull" styles should typically be continuity items that have a predictable rate of sale and have a balanced availability of sufficient volumes of stock from the lowest level to meet the fluctuating demand. The supplier's production planning therefore has to be consistently reliable and flexible to sustain this condition.

The "pull" principle can be illustrated as follows

The automatic replenishment or distribution of products is often performed through the use of sophisticated technical allocation systems and are most suitable for the basic continuity product that have consistent predictable sales patterns and for store displays which are laid out according to a centralised space planning system.

The application needs to be merged with the historical sales data and the planned overall sales going forward. In order to achieve a constant replenishment over time a technique of smoothing is utilised where a weighting factor is applied to sales which deviate from the norm due to an unusual event and in such cases the system will use the adjusted realistic level of sale in the algorithm to derive the most appropriate forward allocations.

In the case where there is a launch of new lines, the new line can be linked to the pattern of a similar current style. The performance of the new styles must therefore be very carefully monitored early on and adjusted if need be to ensure the best size provision as possible.

The manual overriding of calculated allocations at store level should only take place in exceptional circumstances for specific reasons such as unforeseen special events, competitor activity or natural disasters. Often the temptation exists to manually override allocations based on an inherent gut feel and this should be avoided at all costs.

The delivery instruction which is sent to the supplier specifies the quantities that must be picked and packed per item per store by colour and size.

The primary size refers to the commonly designated size of all products such as waist measurements, neck and chest sizes while the secondary size refers to products which have other options of the main primary size such as different leg lengths for trousers or varying cup size options in case of bras.

If automated replenishment systems do not exist or are not very sophisticated it may occur that the actual sales by size do not mirror those as planned. In such cases it is necessary to review the size patterns using a manual technique and alter contract ratios going forward. A special balancing contract must be raised for production of those specific sizes that are short in order to realign the size sales pattern to that of the amended regular contracts going forward. A very clear indication where the size ratio is out of line is where at the end of range launches the left over stocks or reduced stocks are dominated by one or two sizes. If one applies one's mind to the consequence of this, it is a fact that potential sales have gone drastically astray of better selling sizes and profit is consequently not maximised.

In summary, the sad part about poor performers or the lack of stock control, is that especially in the case of high volume continuity styles, the resultant negative impact can be likened to a lingering illness that lives with the buying team until the situation of overstocks of unwanted product is eventually rectified or doomed to the reduced counter. It is therefore critical that where there is a hint of such an evolving scenario that very swift action is taken.

Where there has been above average performance of categories, a situation may arise where the amount stock available is unable to satisfy the requirements of the entire store catalogue. In such instances the predicament that exists is one of how to keep everybody happy. The choice usually boils down to reducing the quantities proportionately across the entire catalogue dependent on the priority of need whereby at least each store sees a piece of the pie before sell outs are experienced. The other option is to take the view to shrink the number of stores that are serviced and best satisfy the stores that are more likely to deliver the greatest volume of sales. In many cases it is not uncommon for twenty percent of the catalogue to deliver sixty to seventy percent of the sales. The selection of the second option will retain the credibility of the customers in the bigger units but will disappoint the many customers across the balance of the stores. A tactic to alleviate severe situations is by choosing a geographical cross section of stores and if an on-line facility exists, to ensure that stock is available at all times that can be ordered via the internet.

The use of digital imaging has helped develop realistic three dimensional representations which enable the product to be placed efficiently on the various types of equipment in the store. Such systems operate at detail size level so in theory a store will never be out of a size as the principle applied is that as the store sells one it gets one. The key to the success of such a system is that the data integrity has to be as accurate as possible. If this is not the case, for example, where the data base is distorted through incorrect barcode ticketing or pilferage will result in allocations being calculated inaccurately. The only means to rectify the data base is to do a disciplined full manual stock count from time to time and update the data base accordingly.

The automatic replenishment or distribution of products is often performed through the use of sophisticated technical allocation systems and are most suitable for the basic continuity product that have consistent predictable sales patterns and for store displays which are laid out according to a centralised space planning system.

Delivery Instruction note example

ORDER NO	12345	DEPARTMENT	Men's Trousers
SUPPLIER	ABC Manufacturer	STYLE NO	5554
DATE	14 March, 2015	DESCRIPTION	Casual cotton trouser

STORES		COLOUR	GREY					
		PRIMARY SIZE	32	34	36	38	40	42
		SECONDARY SIZE	32	34	36	38	40	42
NO	STORE	TOTAL	120	170	160	140	110	100
141	City Centre	250	38	53	50	44	34	66
145	Main Street	200	30	43	40	35	28	53
148	Back Street	250	38	53	50	44	34	66
151	Country Lane	100	15	21	20	18	14	26

REVIEW AND ACTION OPTIONS OF IN SEASON TRADING

Process of comparing the actual performance in relation to the plan

No matter how much time and thought is spent in drafting the strategy and planning forecast it is inevitable that the reality will deviate from what is expected as a result of the volatile internal and external factors that exist at the time. Therefore it is critical to continually review actual performance, analyse the trends and take appropriate action to minimise the risks. Where adjustments are not able to be made to remedy a situation the lessons learnt must be taken on board and banked to be avoided in future trading seasons.

The path to follow in the process of comparing the actual performance in relation to the plan can be outlined as follows

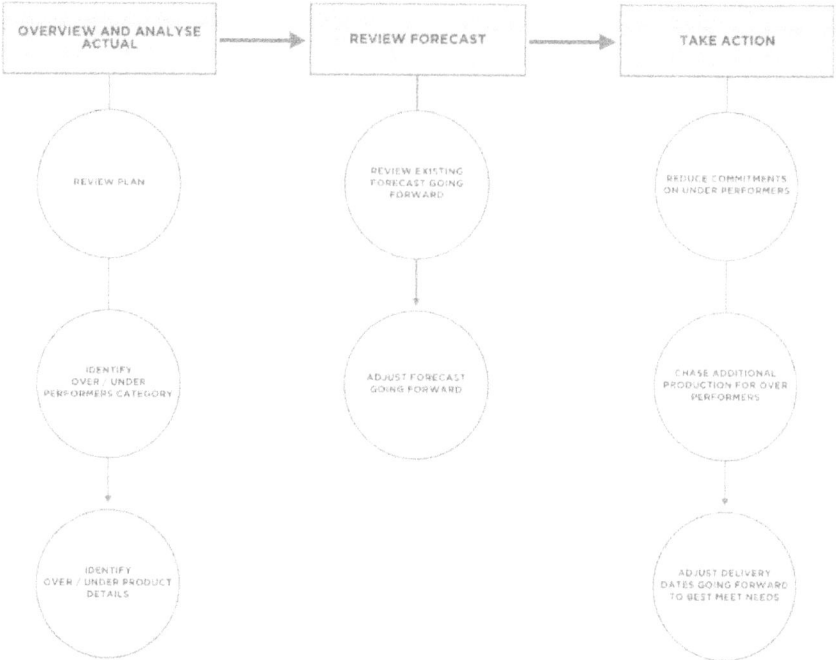

The start point of analysing and comparing the actual performance to the intended plan at a point in time, is to firstly to compare actual sales to date at total departmental level and drill down to product level and based on the result, review the planned sales for the balance of the season.

The potential new sales forecast is then compared to the actual commitment of product in the form of stock on hand at stores, product in transit and that at the supplier as well as the orders in the pipeline to determine the resultant shortage or surplus of stock.

In the scenarios below the assumption is that the department consists of a product which is over performing, another that is under performing and one that is selling to expectation.

The procedure which needs to be followed can be broken down into three distinct activities.

- The recording of the total plan for the season in terms of sales and the planned breaking stocks at the end of the season as well as the current week's performance which has just been completed.

- Based on the comparison of the actual sales to date in relation to that which was budgeted for may require a review of the balance of sales to be achieved and thereby create a revised forecast for the total season. The change in the sales forecast may also then require an adaptation of the planned breaking stocks to reflect the reality of the sales plan.

- Once the realistic revised sales performance has been established, the result then needs to be compared to the total stock commitment and assessed whether there is sufficient stock in the pipeline to achieve the revised targets. If this is not the case, a plan has to be devised in order to determine what action is required to achieve this or conversely there may be a consequent surplus of stock which will have to be reduced.

CONCLUSION

In conclusion the book has not only endeavoured to illustrate how a repository is constructed to house all the very diverse information is housed in such a way that it is easily accessed by the mechanisms that are essential to build and maintain a successful and sustainable fashion retail business.

The structure of the system needs to be robust and flexible to ensure that the data maintains a high degree of integrity and flexibility and represents "one version of the truth" which is so essential to ensure that the flow of the facts and figures is done often seamlessly and speedily in such a way that it remains consistently credible and therefore can continuously be trusted. Failure to achieve this leads to such events often to be blamed simply on "the system" which as a result is often extremely difficult to justify due to the element of uncertainty and mistrust which lingers in the background.

Apart from providing a practical insight into the data management tool the other objective that the book has attempted to illustrate is the broad diverse functions and reporting features across the entire organisation that are dependent on the instrument that effectively links critically to the commercial aspects in such a way that the ultimate strategic objectives are profitably achieved.

There are however crucial elements of stewardship required to guarantee that the future is both successful and sustainable. The demonstration of those elements which are characteristic to a true merchant are outlined below.

Integrity is an absolute unconditional prerequisite that should be evident in all the interactions with all stake holders. In short it is important to uphold the promise of doing what you say you are going to do and maintain a policy of under promising and over delivering.

Passion is clearly illustrated through attributes such as the visible demonstration of the love for the organisation, the product and relationships in such a way that it is contagious and serves as a great motivator to all those who come in contact with a sincere energised trader. An underlying sense of urgency to cope with the continual changes that the marketplace pitches at the retail participants. The response to such events whether they originate from the customers or other competitors needs to be such that it remains composed and the analysis of the situation prepares a clear path of creative action to withstand such onslaughts.

Humility is demonstrated through the focussed retailer from all levels of seniority who listens to customer and sales staff feedback and opinions with an enquiring mind and courteously probes and takes heed of their comments. Often there is a temptation to arrogantly brush disagreeable criticisms aside as being irrelevant but this should be avoided at all costs and every effort should be made to seek to understand and apply different thought processes. This is especially evident in this day and age where the social media has become an indispensable part of day to day living where something that was thought to be initially insignificant can in a matter of hours demand full attention and therefore the need to be sensitive to outside inputs is intensified.

Vigilance and alertness is a precondition to keep the finger on the pulse. An example of this is in the same way that the customer is the reason for the existence of the retailer so are the competitors in a way. The retailer needs to know their rivals intimately and keep watch on them like a hawk. It is so often easy to treat the smaller minnow contestants with contempt and scoff at any hint of threat. However it should be remembered that there are many success stories of such upstart retailers that have rattled the foundations of well-established traders, some of whom are today no more than romantic memories of the past. It is therefore important to admire the boldness of new and emerging entrants and possibly learn from the courageous innovations that many bring with them as they make their way up the ladder in the industry. In the same way there are other competitors who are on the way down the ladder and from them there are many lessons to be learnt as to why they are in decline. In essence therefore the competitors have a valuable input into the sustainability of their counterparts.

Partnerships between the retailer and the supplier is an essential pre-requisite to ensure the success of the retailer. There has to be a circle of trust to promote collaboration and mutual respect. As has been highlighted the only guarantee about change is that there will be change and it is without doubt that the retailers' greatest ally when change happens, whether it be positive or negative, is their source of supply. The support of the supplier through their flexibility and ability to appreciate the need for revolution is vital for the shared destiny and the celebration of success for both businesses through maintaining healthy relationships with the customer.

In summary, having a farsighted view of the overall big picture of the retail environment, with an all-inclusive attention to detail with efficient data management structures and being aware of early warning signs to effectively avoid challenges through the optimised use of the tools, mechanisms and talents at hand is without doubt a key factor in delivering a continued successful and sustainable retail business.

www.ingramcontent.com/pod-product-compliance
Lightning Source LLC
Chambersburg PA
CBHW071816170526
45167CB00003B/1332